I0151552

"Maggie's Kitchen Tails"

Dog Treat Recipes and Puppy Tales To Love

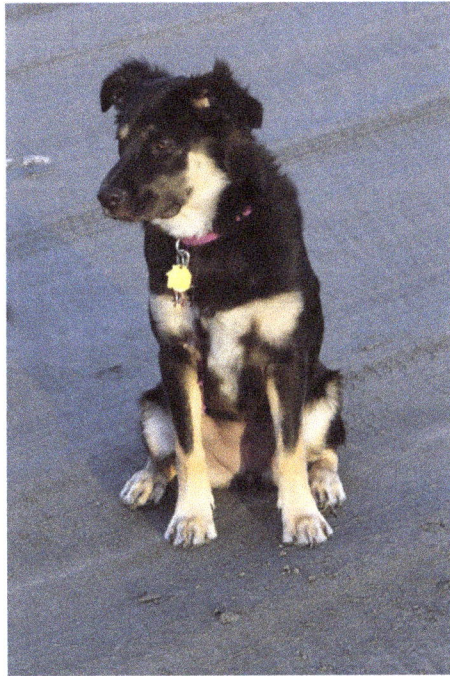

Miss Mamies
Publishing, LLC

Authors:

Rosemary "Mamie" Adkins
Douglas Earl Adkins
Martha Char Love

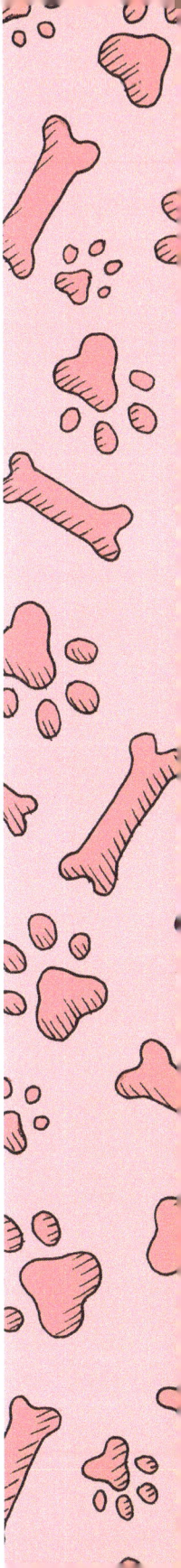

"MAGGIE'S KITCHEN TAILS"
Dog Treat Recipes
and
Puppy Tales To Love

Copyright 2015
Miss Mamies Company, LLC

All Rights Reserved. No portion of this publication may be reproduced, stored in any electronic system, or transmitted in any form or by any means, electronic, mechanical, photocopy, recording or otherwise, without permission from the author. Brief quotations may be used in literary reviews. Coupons only may be photocopied for the sole use of the owner of the book.

Published by:
Miss Mamies Company, LLC

Address all inquiries to:

Rosemary "Mamie" Adkins
5922 Harlow Drive
Bremerton, WA 98312
360-377-9199

ISBN: 978-0-692-60211-9

Library of Congress Control Number: 2015909167

Authors:
Rosemary "Mamie" Adkins
Douglas Earl Adkins
Martha Char Love

Editor: Clayton Bye; Chase Enterprises Publishing
Illustrators: Isabelle Dore & Duncan Fyffe
Cover and Graphic Design: Duncan Fyffe

Please visit our web site at:
http://www.MaggieTails.com

Printed in the USA

READERS' PRAISE

Maggie's Kitchen Tales is a delightful collection of anecdotes and doggie-treat recipes. While the recipes are to cater to the canine palate rather than the human one, children won't get sick if they happen to share one with their four-footed pal as they might with commercial treats. Alas, my dear canine friend is no longer with me and cannot give them a taste test, but I'm sure she would have loved them. The stories are personal experiences with warmth and wit that have a direct connection in an engaging way to why the recipe that follows was developed. It's a fun read, especially for dog lovers, and is for a good cause. I loved it.

R. L. Cherry
Author of *The Morg Mahoney Mysteries*

Maggie's Kitchen Tails is a wonderful collection of recipes and short stories about life with a dog. Many of the recipes originate with the stories told, thus creating interest in the recipes themselves. As a non-pet owner I was surprised to find myself reading every word. A terrific offering dog owners are certain to love.

Clayton Bye
Author, editor and publisher

If you are a dog lover, and even if you don't have a pet, Maggie's Tails is a charming book. It provides wonderful anecdotes about Maggie, Elfie, and Momo while it contains nutritional recipes for all your beloved pets. Maggie, is my hero because I know she has saved Rosemary "Mamie's" life on several occasions and heartily deserves the most delectable snacks in the book; as does your pet. And that includes Silk, the fictional puppy in my book, Deadly Pleasures. Maggie's Tails is a must read for all animal lovers.

Mary Firmin
Author of *Deadly Pleasures*

The love for dogs (and all pets) shines through every page and story of *Maggie's Kitchen Tails*. This book would be a wonderful addition to any pet lover's collection, all the more so because its authors have presented a powerful indictment of animal abuse and its evils. *Maggie's Kitchen Tails* will make you laugh and cry, sometimes on the same page.

John B. Rosenman
Author of *Inspector of the Cross*

Meet Maggie. Lover of a small green chew toy! Oh and did I mention she loves cookies? Yes! Vet accepted cookies and other recipes you can make with your very own pet. Just think of it: dog food for dogs and humans. Or is it human food for humans and dogs? You will also meet a few other dogs with heartwarming stories to tell about their lives and owners (like the luau wedding in the dog park with love cookies). As for the Beefy Beef Heart recipe, I do not recommend it- unless you have paws!

Zak Sherman,
Manager, Silverdale, Wa. Library

SPECIAL THANKS

We, at *Maggie's Kitchen Tails: Dog Treat Recipes and Puppy Tales to Love*, wish to thank each of you for purchasing our book. It is our mission, through donations, to help support the needs of different associations committed to helping dogs enjoy lives with no further abuse, abandonment, fear or starvation.

Our lives have been enriched with our dogs and each day we find so many reasons to be grateful for them. We wish to thank all of the people whose help has encouraged us to write this book; the hard working volunteers that held our hands while we learned how to be better volunteers with the dogs; to all the volunteers that help make the lives happier for the dogs trapped in crates while waiting for a new home and each new volunteer that takes time from their day to give a dog extra love, a ten minute walk and hope.

A special thank you is extended to both Clayton Bye, author, editor and publisher for editing our book, and John Rosenman, author, for his editing and support. Our friendships have surrounded us with love and appreciation of the people in our lives.

The three of us also want to thank our families and our own grand puppies that grace our lives with love and all the wet kisses one could ever want.

Lastly, though she may not be able to read, we all thank our little rescue dog Maggie, for all the great adventures over the last two years, no matter how challenging and for being the inspiration for this book as we knew at the end of each day we all loved one another! We love you Maggie Anne!

Douglas E. and Rosemary "Mamie" Adkins and Martha Char Love

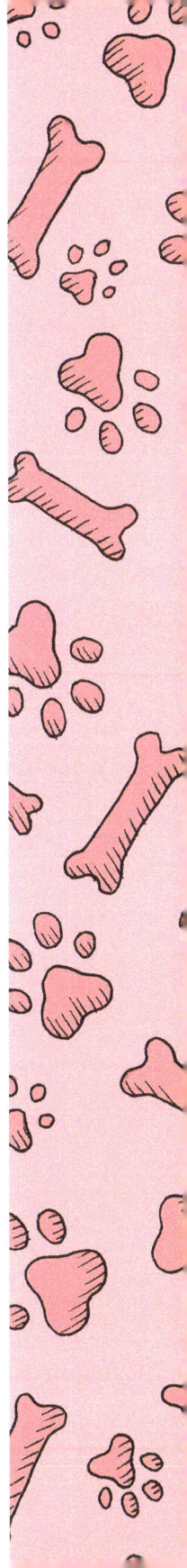

TABLE OF CONTENTS

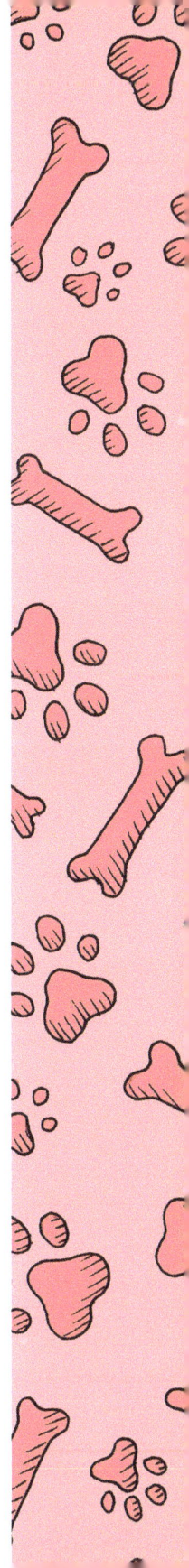

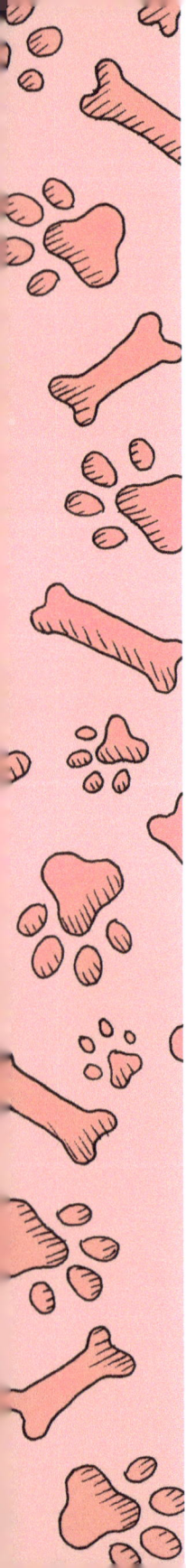

MAGGIE'S KITCHEN TAILS

Dog Treat Recipes
and
Puppy Tales to Love

INTRODUCTION

Meet Maggie Anne. She was rescued from the Humane Society in Silverdale, Washington at the age of eight weeks and has captured our hearts in every way. We are Doug and Mamie Adkins. Because our Maggie was at first difficult to feed, she became the inspiration to bring to you healthy dog food recipes and to share our stories of the adventures of helping an abused puppy return to a world where families love one another.

Another author, Martha Char Love, has joined us in this project. She has an adorable Shih Tzu grand-dog named Momo (below) who has severe food allergies and, thus, special dietary needs. Martha is excited to share her healthy dog treat recipes that she makes for Momo. She will also share some of the wonderful adventures they have had together, along with a few other short puppy tales.

Why We Have Dog Stories in a Recipe Book

We have written this book of dog food and treat recipes with stories of our experiences about our own dogs. It is our hope that our stories will be a pleasant way for you to understand the joy and importance of cooking for your own dog.

We also feel that what is needed to encourage people to help eliminate dog abuse is for them to hear stories of how we can have a warm and reciprocal relationship with the canine family and how abused and rescued dogs can be amazing family members.

In looking into Maggie Anne's past we found that at just a few weeks old she had been beaten, abandoned and tossed away like garbage. We were even told someone bagged her and tossed her into a river. Our sweet puppy was determined to live, however, and her spirit has been one so worth saving. But it was not enough that Maggie wanted to live. At the young age of 8 weeks she faced the surgery all pets endure while in the care of an animal shelter. She was neutered! The poor puppy even had to face a postoperative infection. She almost didn't wake up.

We had been volunteering at the shelter with new admits for surgery, cleaning their pen areas, when they handed her off to us the night before. It was love at first sight and why we went back the day of surgery to help with recovery. We rocked her and held her until she finally opened her eyes. From that moment the dog that had been named Dazzle Me became our little Maggie Anne Adkins.

WRITING OUR BOOK

Moving now to the writing of this book, I can only say it was most enjoyable to write. Not only did we have fun making, testing and documenting recipes we were also able to share short stories about growing up with Maggie. When we went on to invite Martha Char Love to join us as a co-author, we found out she had already developed several special dog treat recipes for Momo. She had also researched the foods best for a variety of needs of dogs while making dog treat recipes for the neighbors in her building. The three of us have worked tirelessly together for both your entertainment and to assist you to understand the benefits of feeding your dogs the very best in nutrition. Within these pages you will find a collection of special dog tales and an assortment of recipes all made with organic humane grade ingredients and filtered water.

I mentioned earlier that Maggie had come to us with her own set of eating problems. It appears that her intestines were not fully developed. Every bite she ate came back and there was no winning with finding foods she could eat. It readily became obvious to us that we had to research foods good for dogs and make all of her food ourselves, including her treats. It was the only way for her survival, and it how this book came to be.

The Recipes

Our first step in creating the recipes in this book was to research what experts say is a healthy diet for dogs. We needed to know what dogs should and should not eat and how much of each food group they need in their daily diet. While we found that experts disagree on nearly everything to do with what makes up a healthy dog's diet, the general consensus is that they need more meat, vegetables and fruits and less (or no) grains. We have included an Appendix A in the back pages of this book that lists the main ingredients that are good for a dog's diet and it is approved by a cross-section of experts on dog nutrition. We have also included an Appendix B with a list of foods that should be avoided in your dog's diet because they may be dangerous for them to digest. Be sure when you make your own dog treats that you consult these appendixes, as well as the expertise of your own vet.

We write this book to foster the health and well-being of all dogs. However, we want you to know that we are donating a portion of the profits of this book to canine rescue centers in hopes of helping dogs who have been abused and/or abandoned. We are also supporting the growing need to re-home animals in hopes that the kill shelters will not find such terrible choices necessary. It's for that reason we have included dog theme stories that relate to both our amazing rescued dogs and to what we might call our "lucky dogs" who have spent most of their lives in a loving and caring family.

While Maggie knew only abuse the first few weeks of her life, Momo and some of her friends knew love and kindness. Still, even though their life beginnings have been quite different, they all share a common need … to be happy and loved.

Maggie has benefitted greatly with the help and support of KARE (Kitsap Animal Rescue and Education), and we have decided that they, as well as the ASPCA and PAWS, will be the charities the three of us support during our launch month, however in 2016 we are looking to donate to several other groups. We also intend to work with shelters everywhere with a fundraising program we have planned.

Our hope is that you enjoy the many stories we have to tell and the recipes all our puppies choose for both treats and meals. Together we three have declared to make a difference in the lives

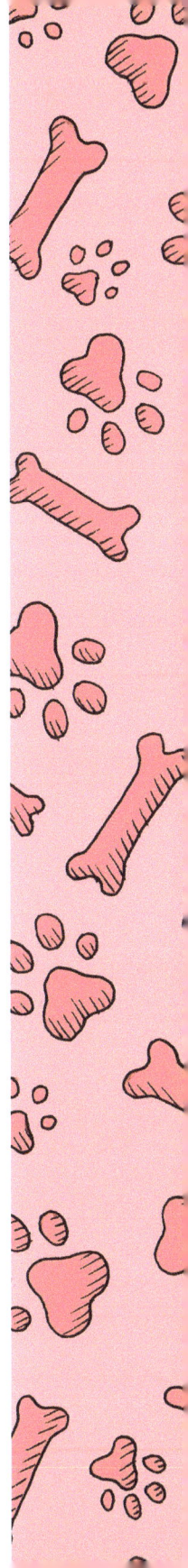

of the many innocent dogs being thrown away each day. This is why we are donating a percentage of the sales for each book sold, in order to help each of them to find a new family home and new beginnings. We thank you for joining us in the support of dog rescue and we sincerely hope you enjoy the puppy tales and dog food recipes in this book.

BENEFITS OF COOKING FOR YOUR DOG

If your puppy has a poor appetite, you may have already tried many types of commercial dog food to find something she/he will eat. We discovered that if we microwave our puppy's dinner for a few seconds, just long enough to arouse an aroma, she would run to her crate for feeding and gobble it down when served. Commercial dog food ads may have you thinking that dogs respond to taste far more than they do. But the sense of smell in dogs is far greater. And for this reason, even if they are already good eaters, cooking your own dog food will give your dogs the great sensing pleasure they so keenly are born to enjoy.

In addition, cooking for your dogs can provide a project that can become a bonding experience for you as a family. It's a special time where you can share compassion while learning to understand the special needs of your pet. If you have young children, you can help them become responsible and caring individuals who better understand that what they eat themselves and what they feed their dog is crucial for better health.

A FEW IMPORTANT TIPS AND NOTES ABOUT DOG FOOD INGREDIENTS

• You can improvise the recipes in this book to fit your own dog's taste and to what you have on hand in the way of ingredients. After consulting Appendix A, you may wish to try substituting the vegetables listed in one of the recipes in this book with whatever vegetables you have on hand in your own refrigerator that you think your dog would like.

• We found that adding a small amount of oat flour to our dog treat recipes makes the dough easier to work with. So if your dog can eat oats, it adds a sweet flavor they may love and it will help you in the cooking preparations. We say small amount because oats are a bit more fattening than other ingredients.

• One rule of thumb—with exception to foods that are only for dogs—is that if you won't eat what you've cooked, then think before you feed it to your furry family member.

• If you plan to make most of the treats for your dogs, seriously consider buying a dehydrator. The reason? The shelf life of dehydrated foods will definitely become longer for the treats and snacks.

• Many experts agree that a small amount of grains in a dog's diet is fine, even nutritious, but it is important not to overdo the grains in your homemade food. Our book offers alternatives. Remember that one of the main reasons for cooking your own dog food is to provide your pet with meals and treats that have less filler and higher nutrient value than commercial dog food. This is particularly important when you are cooking main entrée meals for your dog.

• **Always put safety above all else.** When cooking for your dogs, remember that you are not likely using preservatives found in most commercial dog food, so proper storage is critical. We advise you to consult your own veterinarian if in doubt about any new changes in the diets of your own dogs. Remember that these recipes will yield more than what can be consumed in a few days so, again, watch how you store them. Freeze what can't be used within a few days. Be especially cautious with fish treats and always keep those treats in the refrigerator.

As the three of us present to you our stories and our recipes, it is with joyful hearts that we do so. We so much want you to enjoy each story—as they find their beginnings with the journeys we have taken with our own dogs. There can be no greater joy than to watch a pet emerge as a loving family member who protects you and yours while you too protect them. What better way to show them you love them than to cook nutritious treats and food so their bodies grow strong and their minds and hearts are happy? Together, the three of us, with your help, can make a difference for so many animals abused and unwanted. Please take time to talk, play and nurture your dogs as if they were your children and watch them grow into the being you need in your own lives.

We are proud to be known as doggie parents, and we invite you to send us your stories and share your dog food recipes with us. If we print your story and inspired recipe, we will send you a free signed copy of one of our books or offer you a copy of *Maggie's Kitchen Tails* at a discounted price.

You can send your stories and dog food recipes to: http://www.MaggieTails.com, which is our web site and has a contact us page.

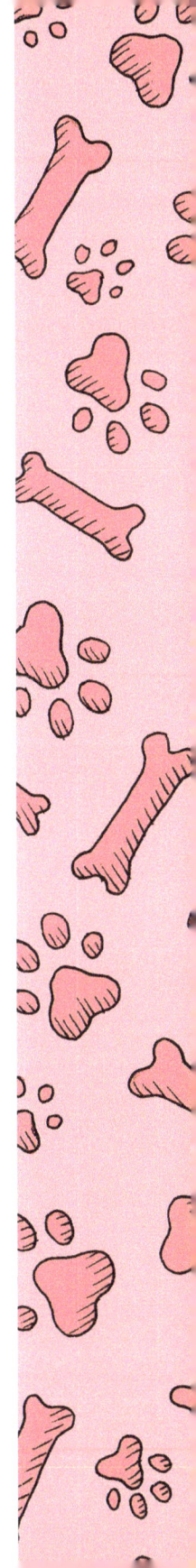

In closing in case you are wondering why a recipe book includes non-fiction stories, we have elected to share the following information about a popular entertainer who devoted his life to animals.

Stories are found to give rise to the urgency of a situation and a need to action that has the power to change both opinions and behavior. This is why so many people loved Jacque Cousteau, because through story (both visual and spoken) he showed us the beauty and feeling of relating to the sea animals that the average person would never otherwise have had the chance to experience. He is often quoted as saying, "People protect what they love." His stories and love of the sea went a long way toward building up human caring about sea life and, in turn, galvanized environmental action. It is our hope to do something of the same with our stories and pictures of some of our most important family members—our dog children!

Won't you help us make this world a better place to be, making a change for so many homeless animals? Please share our book with your family, your friends, as party gifts and to groups that need special fundraising opportunities. Each book sold generates a donation towards making life for many animals a little bit happier.

With Our Greatest Respect,

*The following sections will begin with short stories followed by recipes inspired by the events of each adventure.

APPETIZERS

DOG APPROVED

FOR THE MOST DISCRIMINATING TASTE BUDS.
WE AT MAGGIE'S KITCHEN TAILS WANT ONLY THE
FINEST FOR YOUR FURRY FAMILY AND FRIENDS.
THE APPETIZERS ARE ONES YOU CAN ALSO ENJOY
FOR YOURSELF!

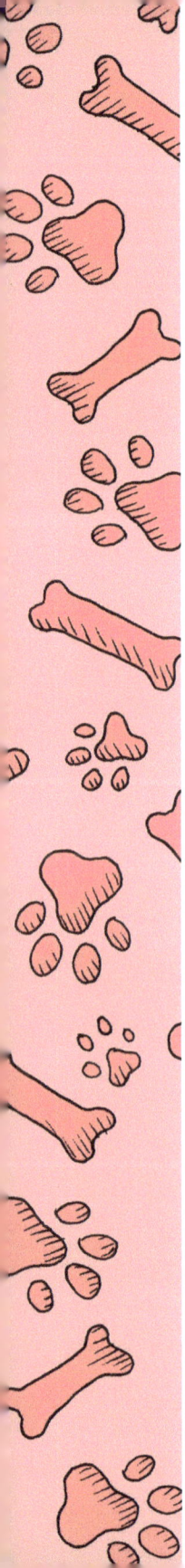

OH HOW WE MISS OUR ANGELS!

by
Rosemary "Mamie" and Douglas Adkins

*L*ife has given us so much joy but without a doubt the most joyful times have been with our daughter and our doggies. Heck, even our grand puppies are there for us to love, and one thing you can count on is they all love us back unconditionally.

We would like to share our poodles first as we take you back to our time with these furry family members.

It all began with a sweet apricot poodle named Coco. Our daughter Kecia and I had been adjusting to our new life after a failed marriage and I wanted her to have someone to love, someone who needed her and who she could call her own. Searching for that special dog, I found Coco for Kecia. It was love at first sight.

Here they both are, Kecia and her special friend, Coco on the beach with my new husband, Doug.

Coco Channel was her fancy name and she certainly did live up to everything we ever wanted for that very special companion. Coco allowed Kecia and me to wrap her in baby blankets and hold her for what seemed like an endless time, telling her all our deepest secrets.

After several years of loving just her, we were thinking about having her spayed to protect her when in heat. On the other hand, I had always heard if a female has a litter they will never stray from home. So, minds made up, we started out to find a male partner for Coco. It wasn't long before we ran across a tiny silver teacup poodle and made arrangements for them to meet.

17

Although Coco did not like the entire affair-from being bred to having puppies; she tried her best to birth the litter and accept them.

All three puppies were such delightful doggies and we loved them all. Each one had their own personalities and we had only begun to see how life was going to change for us all. **Jenger,** the apricot poodle loved to pose for every photograph while **Pierre** just let you do anything with him as his Mother Coco, did with Kecia.

After years of loving our dogs fate took them away from us. Grieving their deaths, we made the tough decision to never go through that kind of loss ever again. But one thing was amiss for so long in our home. It was an emptiness that filled every inch of our lives because the close bond with our furry family members was missing. There was a hole in our hearts where they had all been, and we finally had to admit the only thing that was going to help us recover was to fill our lives with the type of love those feelings came from-the innocent love where no strings are attached, where love is unconditional.

One day we found an advertisement for a female chocolate Labrador that had not been selected from her litter. We decided to set out to meet her. When we arrived at the breeder's home, the puppy had just come from her very first walk on the beach. The fact the ocean is our favorite place on earth was our first clue she would be a great fit for us! After a brief conversation with the breeder the Lab came home with us. On that journey home a name was discussed, and it was easy to think the name Sandy-representing the beach, a place we shared in common and that would be perfect for our newest family member. It was love at first site, and we felt it was meant to be that she was the only puppy still waiting to be adopted; she had waited for us!

Sandy—she earned her name when we first brought her home because of that special walk … her first walk in life being on the beach. It was the very place I found my peace growing up and where we took her often as she was constantly demonstrating her love for it too. She was always splashing in the waters, digging in the sand, exploring what might be in the washed up seaweed and running up and down the beaches as though there were no end to her energy or ours.

It was easy to see with Sandy we had met our match! We were also going to need to be more involved with her daily life if we were to survive puppyhood. Training was our next move. So Sandy and the two of us went to obedience school, and the only problem was that we became her students. All in all, we learned to take walks, Sandy style; eat with her sweet head tilted as if to say "where is my plate" and watch the TV shows she most enjoyed.

Sadly, early on in her life she fell ill to major illnesses that would take her from us. But though she suffered, she never let on. In time, she lost her battle to cancer and passed away before our eyes.

Life, as we had known it, was no more and the total devastation took over our every thought. Again, our home had that emptiness everywhere. Nothing felt good any more. It was soon after her death that we decided to volunteer at the Humane Society (in order to fill that void in our hearts for a few hours each week). But we had no intention to ever bring home any other dog!

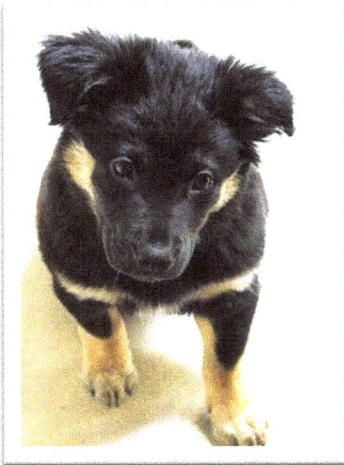

Have you ever made promises to yourself but somewhere in your heart you knew it could never be what you were promising? Well, that is exactly what happened to us. Volunteering was wonderful, but it was also gut wrenching to see so many wonderful animals come in abandoned, dumped or abused. Suddenly these animals were in cages instead of cushy beds at home. Most all had no toy, no food they recognized, no person they could call family and most did not even have their own name any longer because of being abandoned or dumped without any information about themselves. Now how could anyone keep a promise we had made with ourselves after being trained to work with these dogs and see their faces lost and vacant of any hope?

In time, after wanting to take home almost every dog we had hugged, that fateful day arrived. It was as if Sandy had lead us to this little lost and sad soul abused so early in life. There she was—our new family member, at eight weeks of age, just waiting for someone to see that though she had been harmed so badly she still wanted a family and needed someone to love her.

We adopted that puppy and named her **Maggie Anne.** The rest you will learn as you read on through the pages of our book.

Maggie Anne was not the first puppy, duck or stray that had come into Mamie's life. As an abused child herself, she was drawn to the abused animals or those that had 'no one in their life abandoned and alone themselves. Mamie had been raised with Nanny she dearly loved and whom loved her back so she was more than happy to help Mamie create new recipes just for that animal. Luckily her mother also loved dogs so it was allowed to help the strays Mamie brought home. "Life was not so happy growing up, but I had my friends for however long they remained with us" is what Mamie used to tell her closest friends. Years following though not always having her own dog, she would cook for the dogs in the neighbor and became sort of a "pied piper" amongst the dog population! Later in life abuse became one issue Mamie knew she had to deal with so life would be "normal" again. After years of soul searching and facing her demons, she wrote and published her book Reflections of Mamie: A Story of Survival which shared the abuse she endured for decades in hopes of reaching the one person wanting to give up. From that point in her life when she could let go of those demons, still obsessed with solving abuse, she wanted to write with her husband a book which paid tribute to abused dogs in hopes her donations would make a difference.

We did have Maggie for eight months when it was time to take a tiny weekend away celebrating our 25th wedding anniversary, and we could not take her with us. Just a few hours from being gone, our hearts ached even though we knew she was in a very special Day Care named Hidden Creek Dog Farm and a place we had been taking her to play for months … a place she adored while learning social skills, twice a week. How very important it is for you to socialize your dog. The owners there, Heather and Tony McFee, loved our Maggie so we felt safe leaving her. But we were so empty without her.

It goes to show you just how much your furry little family members are so much a part of your lives if you just let them in. They are not a possession but a part of your life. Your dog is not your pet; it's a member of your family. **Loki** (shown on the right) was Maggie's best friend other than the burro that she played with every week.

TONY McFEE, Trainer/Owner

Dr. John Paulson whose life is devoted to animals (with Maggie showing him how much she loves him) says his personal motto is "To live life more like a marathon than a sprint -- and add plenty of rest stops along the way." So Maggie girl, remember all our devotions to keeping you snuggled tight! If afraid just look at our photo and Dr. Paulsen's and you won't be afraid anymore!

Here is the letter we wrote for Maggie while away that we read to her when we returned home:

Oh Maggie, how we miss the sweet loving ways of your wet kisses each morning. Today we are flying away and leaving you for the first time, sad you have grown up enough to be away from home.

Last night you stayed on your own for the first time at Hidden Creek Dog Farm, but we knew if you were lonely or sad Tony would stay with you in the special room where your crate was. A crate filled to overflowing with a cushy bed, toys and

your favorite blanket from home.

Has Tony ever shown you that creek on your walks? Maybe Tony or Heather will tell the creek is named after his dog farm, or maybe they will take you swimming.

As the day begins we sit and reflect about your tiny face watching the oven door waiting for your special cookies to finish baking. On Saturday, I promise we will make those cookies but not until we have so many hugs the cookies can't help but be sweet. Let's call them, *Missin' Maggie Anne Oatmeal Cookies*. What do you think sweet baby?

Mommie and Daddy miss you so much, but we will be thinking about you every day and will come home soon so we can play *Mr. Greenie*. We are so sorry we could not bring you with us, but we are celebrating our 25th anniversary in Las Vegas where you would be too hot. Just know that we will have a party with you too, and we can make up a large appetizer plate for you and your friends.

MAGGIE TODAY!

We will be coming home to hold you, rub your tummy and cuddle your tiny feet in our hands as you kiss our fingers. Maggie, we love you so much and never forget those special markings on your chest mean that an angel is who you are!

Mommie and Daddy

Lip Lickin' Good Trail Mix Appetizers

Dehydrating recipe

Ingredients:

- 2 small zucchinis
- 2 long carrots
- 2 small yellow squash or crooked neck squash
- 1 sweet potato
- ½ # green beans
- 1 teaspoon Ceylon cinnamon
- ¼ cup pure maple syrup
- ½ teaspoon molasses
- 1 teaspoon butter-melted
- ¼ cup extra virgin olive oil
- pinch of sea salt
- 1 teaspoon Italian seasoning
- beef strips: 1 small boneless chuck roast or lean cut beef—2 pounds
- chicken strips-1 large skinless/boneless -about 2 pounds

Directions:

Wash and pat dry all your vegetables.

Using a cutting board slice each vegetable (except the sweet potatoes and carrots) in 1/8" thick slices and add to a medium size bowl. Use a separate bowl for each vegetable (or prepare one at a time)

For sweet potatoes cut each potato in half lengthwise and then cut them in quarters lengthwise as well. Slice each section in thin steak style strips with half of the potatoes. With the other half of sweet potato cut it in half and with one quarter use a potato peeler making lengthwise peel pieces to add another look for the trail mix and finally the last quarter cut into 1/8" thick slices. This may seem like a lot of work but for your special family member, these treats last a long while and variety is always good when the treats are so healthy.

Repeat the same idea for the carrots except slice one carrot in 1/8" thick slices and with the other carrot, again use a potato peeler and peel the carrot for that different appearance and texture for your canine family member.

Seasoning for carrots and sweet potatoes:

Mix in a small microwaveable bowl add 1/4 cup maple syrup, 1teaspoon melted butter, 1 teaspoon Ceylon cinnamon, 1/2 teaspoon of molasses and microwave for 15 seconds. Drizzle this mixture over both batches of sweet potatoes and mix well. Depending on the size of the vegetables used, you may need to make a bit more of the mixture to drizzle. Note: it is to be used sparingly, and it's only used for that special treat flavor.

As you have each batch completed, lay them in a single layer on the dehydrating trays (be sure to use the mesh liner for the tray—if available) and follow the manufacturer's instructions for drying.

REMAINING VEGETABLE SEASONING:

Cut the squash, zucchini in 1/8" thick slices and cut green beans in half adding them in separate bowls to keep separated.

BLEND: For each batch of vegetables

1/4 cup extra virgin olive oil, a pinch of sea salt (optional-not needed), 1 teaspoon Italian seasoning. Warm in microwave for 20 seconds. Remove from microwave and drizzle the mixture over the vegetables tossing them so they are coated well.

BEEF AND CHICKEN PREPARATION: These are made the following day from vegetables as they cannot be dried together due to temperature differences.

We add these in our trail mix and also separately as appetizers.

Slice beef strips as though you were doing so for a stir fry-very thin. It does not matter that each piece is exact but try to get them the same in thickness of 1/8" and about 4 to 6 inches in length.

Slice chicken breast using only boneless/skinless chicken breast into thin strips about 1/8" thick or less if possible and the length of the breast.

Try to keep both beef and chicken the same width and length to help in drying time.

BLEND: For each batch of beef and chicken

1/4 extra virgin olive oil, pinch of sea salt (optional-not needed), 1 teaspoon Italian seasoning. Warm in microwave for 20 seconds. Remove from microwave and drizzle the mixture over the beef tossing so they are coated well but not saturated.

Remove from bowl and lay on dehydrator trays as for the vegetables also using the mesh tray liners.

Again follow the manufacturer's directions for drying.

After dried, allow to cool before removing and store in an airtight container and refrigerate. Keep out only what can be used in a few days and freeze the balance-remember safety always comes first when not using preservatives.

Your family canine member will love you for these enough to share each bite with you!

Remember these are treats so please do not overfeed. ENJOY!

MAGGIE'S NEW BUDDY
by
Rosemary "Mamie" Adkins

Only 30 years in difference!

Adopting a new puppy, parents soon learn there is much to do in order for training to make a difference in everyone's life … both the puppy and the parents!

Socialization becomes a critical part of training, but we had no idea little Miss Maggie Anne would find it such a big influence in her life that it would impact the direction of our daily routines. Her biggest social event occurred on her first walk after a training session that had left her wanting to make friends and have a playmate.

It happened when Maggie was about twelve weeks old, but we never would have expected that her new buddy would be many times larger than her own pint size. *It was a full grown burro no less!* Right out of the gate, these two struck up a chatter that only they understood. Actually, they were quite taken with one another. The burro would "heehaw" as burros are known to do and little Maggie would respond with her own best rendition of burro-ese which started out as "AWWWWWW!" Even more fascinating, Maggie decided that most of her daily walks were to go in the direction of the burro's field. We always followed her lead to accommodate their meet ups. Whenever we approached Mr. Burro's field, Maggie hurried to call him to the fence.

Maggies new and improved burro-speak has now evolved into something close to "EEEEE-AWWWW!" which never fails to bring him rushing to the fence ... and that's when the kisses begin! Of course it may have a little to do with Maggie sharing her special treats with her new friend every day we walk in that direction. Buddy gleams and heehaws as he enjoys his cookie treats. So move over Budweiser, Maggie makes special friends too!

DOUG'S CORNER

WE WENT TO a LOCAL EATERY WITH a FRIEND - HaD a NICE DINNER - GOT HOME aND I WALKED aROUND THE CaR TO LET MaMIE OUT (BEING THE GENTLEMAN THaT I aM) THE aTTaCHED PICTURE IS WHaT I FOUND. THE CLOSURE ON HER PURSE HaS a MaGNET aND WHEN SHE HaD PUT HER PURSE DOWN ON THE TaBLE aT SOME TIME - THE FORK aTTaCHED ITSELF TO HER PURSE. MaKES ME WONDER WHaT THE PEOPLE WERE SaYING WHEN WE WaLKED OUT OF THE RESTaURaNT WITH a FORK aTTaCHED TO HER PURSE.!!

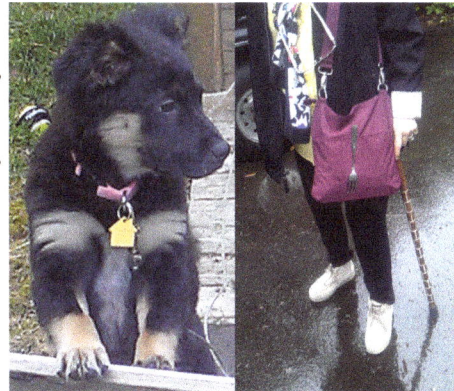

Oh Mommie
Why is that fork on your purse?

27

Buddy's Sweet Potato Chips

This one can either be used in a dehydrator or in an oven at 200⁰F. For timing consult your oven or dehydrator instruction sheets as they will vary. Expect them to take 8 hours or longer.

Ingredients:

- 2 large organic sweet potatoes
- ¼ cup molasses
- ¼ cup maple syrup
- ¼ teaspoon cinnamon

Directions:

Thoroughly wash the sweet potatoes

Slice potatoes as thin possible or use a potato peeler for variety

Blend the ingredients together

On a plate using a pastry brush, lightly coat each piece

We like to coat half, leave ¼ plain and sprinkle lightly with cinnamon the other ¼ (for variety).

This is a healthy treat for everyone. Your pet does not need a lot of sugar -use sparingly when brushing with mixture

Enjoy-share and gift package for the furry friends in your life.

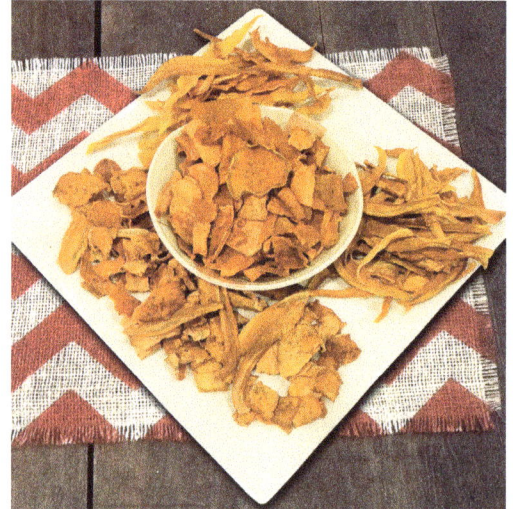

Miss Moon and Her Turkey Friend Oop

by
Martha Char Love

Once upon a time about 40 years ago, we lived in an old fashion farm house in Florida. It had a long porch on the front and also one on the back of the house, and it sat square in the middle of three acres of yard that was completely fenced in. Now I suppose you could say that we had a small farm because we had chickens, guineas, ducks, a female turkey named Oop, two young iguanas named Cheech and Chong, a cat named Larry, and two dogs named Mr. Tree and Miss Moon. Most of the animals preferred to each do their own thing with their own kind in their own little territory of the farm, with Cheech and Chong being separated from the rest of the animals on the farm, as they lived in a large cage that hung on the front porch in the summer and on a table in the living room in the winter. But there was one exception to the rule and that was the great friendship between Miss Moon and Oop.

Miss Moon was a small black lab and loved to make her rounds to check on all the inhabitants of the farm (including the humans). She would make these rounds about four or five times a day in between her naps on her favorite rug in the kitchen. And often Oop could be seen walking about five feet behind Miss Moon on her rounds as she followed dutifully like a deputy behind a sheriff. After checking the chicken house, the ducks in their tub, and circling the front yard to find the guineas, Moon would return to the house. She had figured out a method of her own to open the back screen door to the house and to come into the kitchen. The Turkey would, of course, scoot in right behind Miss Moon and they would stroll throughout the house, look around at us humans, and go out the back door where the iguanas were housed. That pretty

much completed their mission. We were never sure that we really wanted a turkey walking through the house several times a day, but the two friends were too busy and too cute to ever stop.

If someone came to our gate, Miss Moon and Mr. Tree would run out of the house or from wherever they happened to be in the yard so that they could greet a family member or bark at a stranger. And who do you think ran right along behind them? Yes, you guessed it! Oop! We always imagined that Oop was under the impression that she was a dog too or that perhaps she thought the dogs were turkeys like her. At any rate, I write this little story to say that many species of animals have been known to be friends with dogs (including elephants), and some are very unlikely combinations at that. Dogs are truly amazing animal friends and like our son once said at a very young age as he looked up at us while petting a neighbor's dog, "Dog makes life good!"

Almond Butter Balls

Since almonds are good for most dogs, I wanted to try a version of cookies that could be enjoyed as a substitute for peanut butter cookies (particularly for dogs that are allergic to peanuts). These turned out to be loved by all the dogs I cook for, and I think you can count on these to delight your dog's palette. You also might want to try doing what my neighbor Mary does to further exercise her dog Kona: she takes the Almond Butter Balls and throws them for her dog to retrieve and eat. Kona always waits until after she retrieves her treat and brings it to Mary's feet before gobbling it up. I'm pretty sure not all dogs would be that obedient!

Ingredients:
- 2 tablespoons blueberries (mashed)
- 1/2 almond flour
- 1/2 cup oat flour
- 1/2 teaspoon dried parsley
- 6 tablespoons almond butter
- 1/2 teaspoon olive oil
- 1 egg

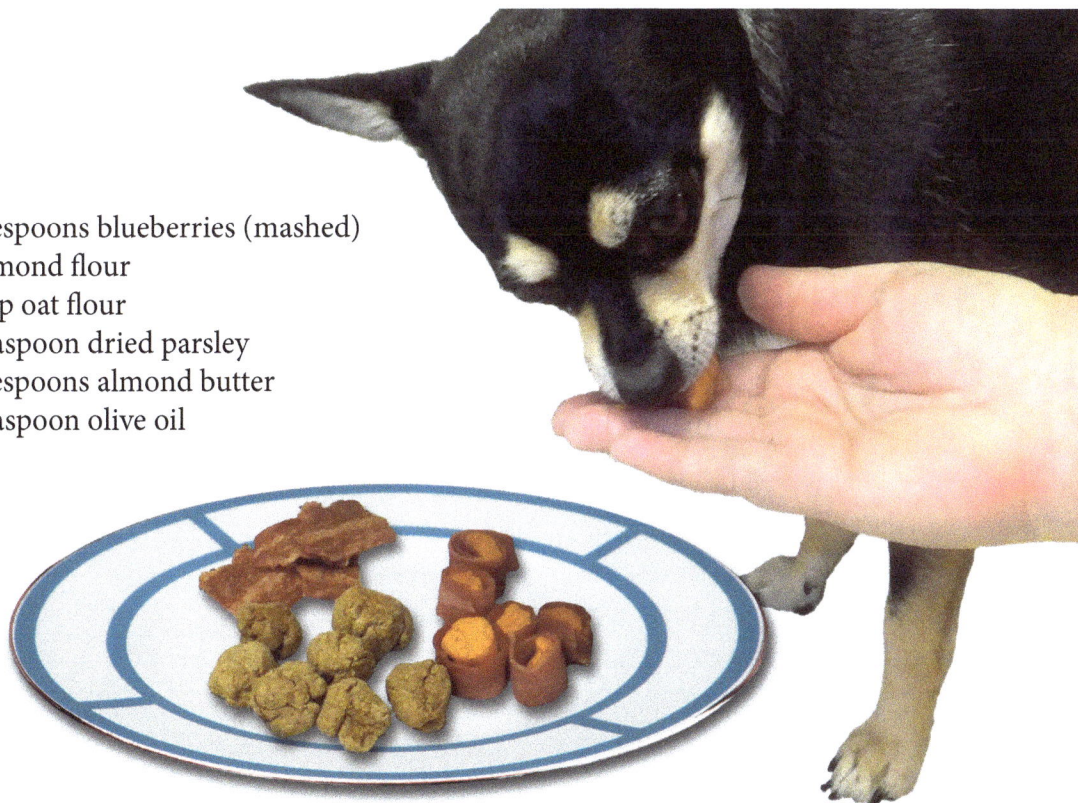

Aloha eats Almond Butter Balls at her fifth year birthday party!

31

Directions:

Preheat oven to 325° F.

Add and mash blueberries in large bowl.

Add oat flour, parsley, almond butter, oil and egg and knead until well combined.

Let set in bowl for 10 minutes.

Using wet hands roll batter into balls using about 1 tablespoon for each ball (less for small dogs). Place on oiled baking sheet.

Bake 20 minutes.

Cool them. And then roll them or hand serve them to your favorite canine.

DOUG'S CORNER

WE WENT OUT FOR A LITTLE WALK RECENTLY AND MET UP WITH "SOMEONE" ALONG THE WAY. MAGGIE JUST STARED AT THE CAT. DIDN'T BARK OR GROWL BECAUSE I DON'T KNOW THAT SHE REALLY KNEW WHAT IT WAS AND THAT SHE WAS SUPPOSE TO CHASE THEM. IN FACT, AS WE WALKED AWAY, THE CAT STARTED FOLLOWING US. SIAMESE CATS ARE STRANGE AND UNIQUE IN BEHAVIOR. I GREW UP WITH SEVERAL AND LOVED THEM ALL. ONE ACTUALLY RETRIEVED THE CRUMPLED UP CIGARETTE PACKS THAT MY MOTHER WOULD THROW AND BRING THEM BACK TO HER. I WAS HOME ONE TIME, WHILE I WAS IN THE NAVY, AND WATCHED THIS CAT GET UP ON THE BACK OF A STUFFED CHAIR THAT WAS NEAR THE BEDROOM DOOR, AND ATTEMPT TO USE HER PAWS TO OPEN THE DOOR KNOB.

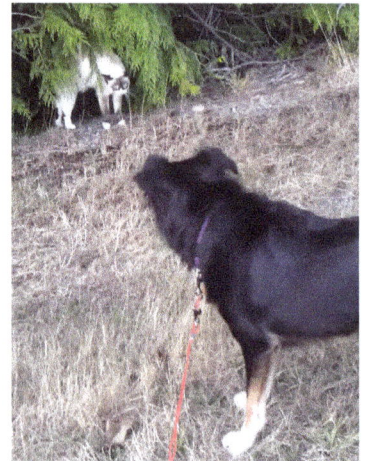

Basic Instincts

by
Rosemary "Mamie" Adkins

It has been heartening to see Maggie's natural instincts develop, especially in the face of potential danger. That is not to say that her curiosity doesn't still get the best of her on occasion, but she knows that we are there to protect her which encourages her to explore, even if she has to take some extra precautions. As we were trekking together on one fine walk, we were interrupted by the sound of loud barking that came from somewhere behind the bushes. To me, it sounded like loud strikes of thunder and a million bolts of lightning but Maggie had her own special way of handling this threat. Our little girl did not run but instead, stopped, sat on the pavement and tucked herself between daddy's legs as if to say "protect me" … voila, *problem solved!*

It got even better when her protective instincts began to click in, especially when confronted by an unknown, potentially nasty little critter along the way. When this happens, she takes a rigid stance and attempts to scare it away. Her sense of obligation toward us is developing in a beautiful way and when we reward her, she knows that she has done her duty toward us. After all, she feels obligated to protect Mommy and Daddy. Of course, those are the times that she appreciates making it safely home again where she sits quietly on Daddy's lap and then switches to Mommie's without moving but a few a muscles.

As Maggie Anne continues to grow, we take our greatest pleasure just watching her prance proudly down the street, looking so fine with her expressive brown eyes and shiny black coat. Training has taught us to reward her when she checks in with us by returning for face to face contact. Of course she has learned what puppies must learn and that is to enjoy the rewards of good behavior such as a loving pat on the head, getting a relaxing belly scratch and a healthy doggie treat that we bake especially for her.

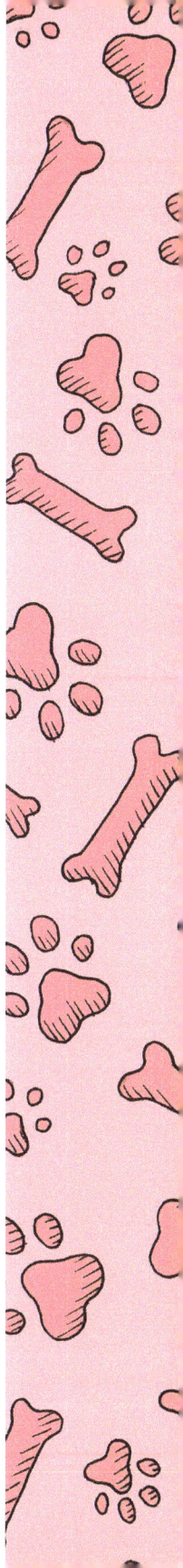

Swimin' Fantail Surprise Appetizers

Ingredients:

- 15 mini fillo dough shells
- 15 medium shrimp
- 1 box low fat cream cheese (we use Laughing Cow Cheese but the whipped cream cheese is affordable and easy to use)
- 1 small fresh mango peeled and diced small or thinly sliced

Directions:

On a cookie sheet place your Fillo Dough mini shells

Cut the shrimp

Add 1/3 slice from a wedge of Laughing Cow Cheese in each cavity being careful not to crush the shells

Now add the shrimp on top of each shell so it rests on the cheese

Top with a diced or thinly sliced piece of mango

Place on a serving plate and share them with your canine family member. Save a few for the best friend. That could be you too!

Yields 15

Hint:

If you want to adapt this recipe so you have more to share without higher cost, cut the shrimp in half lengthwise. Purchase 2 boxes of 15 count of Fillo shells This will yield 30 in case you would like to serve half for yourself and the other half for your family canine and friends.

Traveling with Dragon

by
Martha Char Love

When our son was age six he loved to awake at five am and go around and "collect all the dogs" in our small neighborhood and take them for a walk a little ways up the mountain behind our house in Northern California. He had acquired permission from the four neighbors whose dogs he walked at this early, chilly hour, and the dogs ranged in size from a Cocker Spaniel to a large dog named Max, who was a black Retriever. There was a dry creek bed that ran behind our house, and just on the other side of it was a short street where the dogs lived. Each morning, he would wait until I had quickly brewed my morning coffee, and then he would bust out the back door. I needed something warm to hold onto while watching him from the back porch as he made his rounds gathering the dogs.

Now the one dog he loved the most was Max, who we called Old Max because he walked very slowly like an old man and we thought he was a very old dog. One sad day, Old Max went missing. By afternoon we became very concerned and talked with his owners about his whereabouts. Unfortunately, his owners were not concerned about having him return and said that if we wanted to check the animal shelter, we could have him if we paid the fine to get him out. With that, we nearly flew to the shelter. And it was there, among the daily pickups, that we found Old Max. We paid the fine, and when we brought him out to the car, he perked up and pranced like a young stallion. At that very moment in time, we all decided to give him a new name and called him Dragon. Later, we found that he was only a year old and had actually seemed old and slow because he was somewhat depressed from lack of attention by his owners. He was never depressed again and always held his head high and pranced around with the dignity of royalty.

Now, what we didn't know about Dragon was the one thing that perked him up above all else was to ride in a car. He most likely even enjoyed the ride to the pound and may have hopped in their van voluntarily. We left just a few days after we rescued him for a long cross country trip to visit relatives in Georgia. Dragon was in his element riding along with us. You have never seen a happier dog with his face to the wind staring at the USA as we went on our way.

This tale has an ending that was a bit sad for us, but not to him, so we suspect it was all just as well. Upon our return home from our trip, a few months passed and since we did not go for another long trip, Dragon began to have a wonder lust for the road. He kept running off to a neighbor's house and jumping in the van of their friend who was visiting and preparing for a long road trip. We really had little say in the matter as Dragon had made his decision to go along. He jumped in the car to stay and was ready to roll. The friend was happy to have him as a companion, and we agreed it was best for Dragon's happiness. We handed his new owner a large bag of Dragon's favorite Turkey Bacon Biscuits and hugged him goodbye. That was the last time we saw Dragon, but we know he was happy as a gypsy traveler and he loved his new home on the road.

Joy Jump-Up Turkey Bacon Biscuits

Another favorite food of Aloha's is turkey bacon biscuits. This is what I cook for Aloha when I am dog sitting for her while her mom is away. The bacon smells coming from the oven keep Aloha happy and anticipating the bacon biscuits. Otherwise she sits sadly at the door awaiting her mom's return. Bacon is about the only thing that can change her mood no matter who is or is not present. We think these bacon biscuits also will make some nice hors d'oeuvres at doggie birthday parties, providing you make enough of them so there are plenty to go around for all the dogs to have their own separate little plateful. Have you ever met a dog yet that did not jump up for bacon?

Ingredients:

- 2 teaspoons olive oil or coconut oil
- 2 tablespoons water
- 1 medium egg
- 1 cup buckwheat flour
- 1 teaspoon flaxseed meal
- 1 pinch of baking soda
- 1 pinch of baking powder
- 1 medium cooked sweet potato
- 12 strips of cooked turkey bacon (I use the microwave so not to lose any flavor. Place 3 or 4 strips at a time on a plate with 2 pieces of paper towels on bottom and top. Microwave 2 minutes.)

Directions:

Preheat oven to 350^{0}F.

Mix oil, water, and egg together in a mixing bowl.

Add the flour, flaxseed meal, baking soda, baking powder and knead until dough softens a bit.

Cut the cooked bacon strips into halves. Now you have 24 pieces.

Take about ½ teaspoon sweet potato and roll into a ball. Place the sweet potato roll in the center of a bacon half strip and roll up the piece. If you have a medium to large dog, this will be good size for a treat. If you have a small dog, cut the roll up in half.

Now you will cover the bacon with batter. Scoop about a ½ tablespoon of batter (less batter) for the small dog treats) in your hand and cover each rolled strip into a ball, hiding the bacon in the center with just a tiny bit peeking out.

Place the ball onto a lightly greased cookie sheet and press it down slightly to flatten into a biscuit. Repeat for all pieces of bacon. You should end up with 24 biscuits for large dogs and 48 for small dogs (unless you ate some of Rover's bacon along the way!).

Bake approximately 15 minutes at 350^{0}F.

38

HAPPINESS NEVER FELT SO GREAT!

Our Angel girl, Maggie
by
Rosemary "Mamie" Adkins

Destiny spoke to us the day we met sweet Maggie Anne. We were getting our little puppy fix while volunteering at the local Humane Society when we were drawn to her sad little eyes which spoke volumes about her need for love and of the abuses she had suffered in the first few weeks of her life. We took her home and the rest is history for us all!

Maggie is our special little character who never fails to take me back in time. And how does she do that? Well, she inspires us much in the same way that sentimental music can take one back to memorable times from the past. Music has that special effect for me, as when I was growing up, I escaped unpleasant reality by identifying with music and lyrics-allowing me to escape or dream of happier times.

We take our daily walk with Maggie but she has way more energy than we do so we try to inspire ourselves with happy music as we walk down the street together. Can you imagine two seniors walking the dog while singing *Do Wha Diddy Diddy,Dum Diddy Do*? Well, that would be Doug and I nearly every single day. Yes, me…the one who has not walked anywhere in years other than in a shopping mall!

We especially enjoy our mini vacations at the beach, but each step has been a challenge as we attempt to educate our baby. Maggie Anne has a curious mind and you can easily read her thoughts or intentions. Her eyes light up like sparkling fires on a quiet beach at night especially when she catches sight of any little being that might make a fun playmate.

She is so amazing strutting her stuff as she closely watches the seagulls while wondering why they don't want to play! What she doesn't know is that these baby gulls are closely guarded by their parents who are always nearby, just as we protect her from any threats that may come her way. This is when our homemade doggie treats come in very handy.

On one such occasion, in her quiet fashion she suddenly lunged at the birds in a playful action. Thankfully, her Daddy had a tight grip on the leash and pulled her back in closely to him. All I could do was shout, "Maggie, come back!" Just then, I noticed a huge flock of birds in flight heading in formation straight toward Maggie and Doug. There had to be hundreds of them and I could only think, "Oh my gosh, now what are we going to do?" Maggie and Doug were running at great speed through the swallow waters as it splashed across Maggie's face and soaked Doug's pant legs. The waves were coming in furiously now at high tide but all I could do is yell over and over to look out.

Anxiously I threw treats at the birds to distract them. Now we all know that sea gulls cannot resist food of any description and seeing this flock dive bomb my offerings was a relief that they enjoyed those morsels rather than attack Maggie and Doug. However, Maggie did approach a bit more cautiously so she could share in the treat fest and it seemed to convince the birds that she meant no harm. Finally we returned to the warmth and security of our motel room where we succumbed to our exhaustion after this vigorous Maggie workout. A long nap was to be our reward.

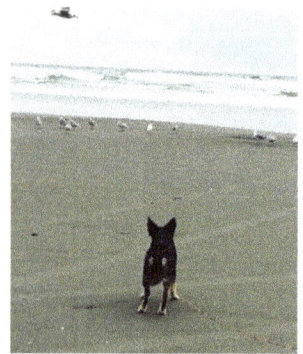

Now my mind is filled with memories of our many eventful walks which never fail to bring those happy lyrics to mind… *Do Wha Diddy Diddy, Dum Diddy Do!*

Reflecting back, Maggie has met so many dear friends on her daily outings. Even when we vary the route, she seems to be on a mission to make new friends. I must admit that Doug and I make a pretty strange sight as we head out, weighted down with our snack bags, water bottles and paper towels! Geez – and let's not forget her poo bags, for her business along the way. In a loving way, these daily outings remind me of early motherhood! Who can forget that 'carry-all' diaper bag filled to meet every eventuality? Well – it's not much different than that.

So here we are,
TOGETHER FOREVER,
"We're so happy and that's how we're gonna stay, singing
Do Wha Diddy Diddy, Dum Diddy Do!"
At least that's the plan.

Rollin' Along Tuna

Ingredients:

- 4 cups tuna , drained
- 16 ounces low fat cream cheese
- ¼ cup finely chopped fresh parsley
- ¼ cup diced almonds
- ¼ cup sunflower seeds-NO salt

Directions:

Mix all ingredients together and drop by teaspoons making an impression with your thumb or a fork and lay them on parchment paper fitted to a plate or small tray for the refrigerator. Refrigerate until set up. These can also be placed in a freezer so your furry friend can have something cold to eat.

Serve with favorite dog crackers. Should be refrigerated or frozen to maintain freshness

TREATS

MAGGIE'S KITCHEN TAILS
DOG TREAT RECIPES AND PUPPY TALES TO LOVE
OUR TREATS ARE ALL MADE FROM HUMAN GRADE
INGREDIENTS AND TESTED FOR THEIR GREAT TASTE! TRY
OUR RECIPES FOR THAT VERY SPECIAL TRAINING TREAT
OR WHEN YOU JUST WANT TO SAY I LOVE YOU.

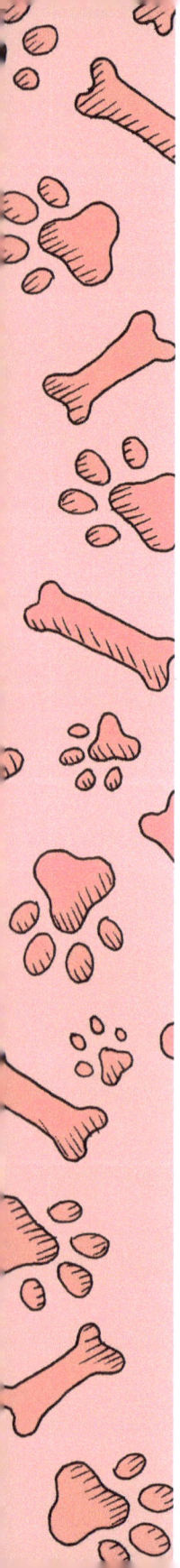

The Tale of Momo and the Bananas
by
Martha Char Love

One day when Momo was a little puppy, my son and daughter-in-law brought home a big bunch of ripe yellow bananas and put them in their banana holder on the kitchen table. Have you ever seen a banana holder? It looks like a curved hook on the end of a stick. When Momo came into the room, she looked at those bananas hanging on the holder and started barking like crazy. They tried to calm her down but she just kept barking and barking, like an unwanted stranger was in the room. After a while, they decided to introduce her to a single banana in hopes this would calm her. But when they pulled off a banana from the bunch and brought it closer to her, she ran under the sofa and hid. It seemed that no matter what they did, she was afraid of bananas!

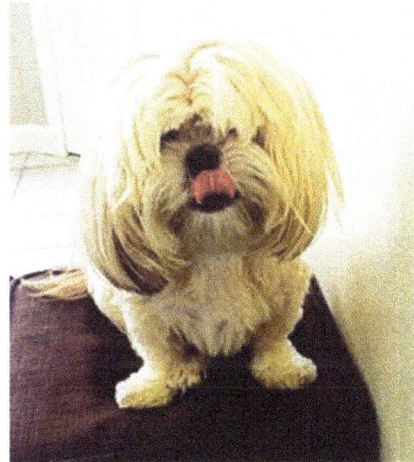

Momo awaiting a banana pancake treat!

When she was almost one year old, Momo was still afraid of bananas, barked at them and would still run and hide from them. My son and his wife had long given up on trying to get her to like bananas. One day by some luck as they were sharing one themselves, they accidentally dropped a piece of banana on the floor. To their surprise, Momo sniffed it and then gobbled it right up. Who would have thought to feed her one? But it turns out that bananas, eaten in moderation, are a healthy food for dogs and provide plenty of energy, along with loads of amino acids, electrolytes, minerals, vitamins B6 and C, potassium, fiber and manganese. Momo loved eating them from that day on and never barked at them again. In fact, today, if you start peeling a banana, she will come running over to you in hopes of getting a piece. Bananas are now her friends!

Momo is allergic to many food ingredients contained in commercial dog foods. She was given the Liquid Gold Allergy Test (which claims to have no false positives) and it was found that she is highly allergic to peas, barley, corn and rice—as well as turkey, lamb and pork—all found in many commercial brand dog treats and food. We have found that there are many dogs, both rescued dogs and dogs like Momo who are bought from excellent breeders, that have food allergies, and thus they have special dietary concerns. But if you cook for your dog, it is not hard to find some delicious homemade treats just right for your little angel. Thus, the treats with banana as an ingredient were created especially for Momo. She loves them and we think your dogs will love them too!

DOUG'S CORNER

TODAY WE HAD GONE DOWN TO THE CHEVROLET DEALER (THERE WAS A RECALL FIX ON OUR CAR). UPON RETURNING, I STARTED FOR THE STREET TO GET THE MAIL AND MY WIFE (I WON'T MENTION ANY NAMES - MAMIE) EXCLAIMED IN TERROR (OK, MAYBE DISGUST) THAT NEAR OUR GATE WAS ONE OF THE LARGEST, UGLIEST SLUGS SHE HAD EVER SEEN AND ASKED ME TO COME BACK AND GET RID OF IT SO OUR DOG WOULDN'T GET INTO IT. I CAME BACK TO SAVE THE DAY. LOOKING WHERE SHE SAID, I DIDN'T SEE ANYTHING. SHE SAID "RIGHT THERE". I LOOKED AGAIN AND ASKED "DO YOU MEAN THIS LEAF"? SHE SAID "WHAT?" THE TERROR HAD BEEN AVERTED. SEE THE PICTURE TO THE RIGHT. I GUESS YOU COULD MISTAKE IT FOR A SLUG. BUT I DID STILL SAVE THE DAY! I KILLED THE LEAF AND REMAINED THE HERO.

No-grain Banana Puppy Pancakes

This banana pancake recipe is Momo approved and is one of her favorite treats. She loves to do tricks for her banana pancakes, like lay down, roll over and then sit waiting for another treat. Remember, we like to use all human grade food ingredients in our recipes, including organics whenever possible.

Ingredients:
- ¼ cup mashed banana
- 2 tablespoons unsulphered Blackstrap Molasses
- 2 tablespoons water
- 1 tablespoon olive oil
- 1 cup buckwheat flour *
- 1 teaspoon flaxseed meal
- ⅛ teaspoon baking soda
- ⅛ teaspoon baking powder

*Did you know that buckwheat is a berry, not a grain!

Directions:

Preheat oven to 350^0F.

Mix banana, molasses, water, and olive oil together in a medium size mixing bowl.

Add the flour, flaxseed meal, baking soda, baking powder and stir until dough softens a bit.

With lightly wet hands, scoop a tablespoon into your hands and roll in a ball.

Place the ball onto a lightly greased cookie sheet and press the ball down to flatten into pancake, only ⅛ to ¼ inch in height. (This recipe makes about three cookie sheets worth or four dozen.)

Before baking, press a cookie cutter into the center of each to indent a cute shape in each treat (optional).

Bake approximately 20-22 minutes, (25 minutes for crunchier).

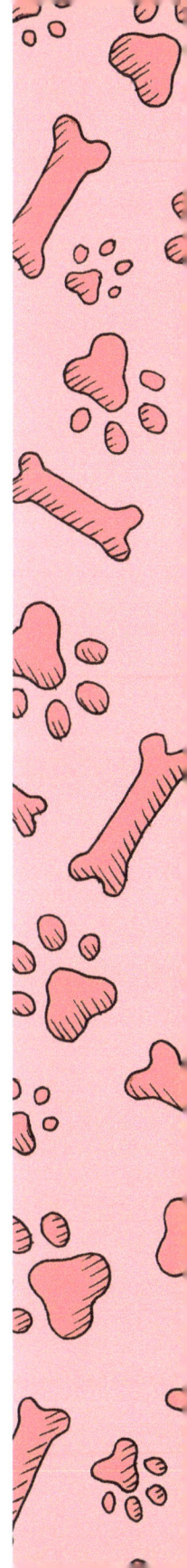

Pierre Stays Home

by
Rosemary "Mamie" Adkins

Imagine having three puppies being born right before your eyes and having to hand feed the puppies when the mother wanted nothing to do with her babies. This sweet Mommie, a toy poodle, was just not well enough to feed them so we did.

When the time came she gave us two all black males and one apricot female. Eight weeks of day and night feedings with our hearts full of love watching these precious lives begin from the time they were so small they fit in the palm of our hands to becoming full grown loving pets, and giving back so much!

Each day as they grew we watched as their little eyes opened and peaked back at ours. It was pure heaven to be there watching each breathe they drew, to help them learn to walk and to teach them each new phase in their lives, as though they were our children.

That was the problem: three puppies all special in their own way. We had bred the mother so she could have a litter of puppies before having her spayed but now we faced having either four poodles or selling them. A good friend decided she wanted one of the black puppies, and we decided to sell the other male and keep the apricot female (since she looked so much like her Mommie).

One now gone and one left to sell but how? We had already named the little black puppy Pierre and loved him dearly. We made two failed attempts to have him adopted out but each time the placement was a mistake. One almost owner changed her mind and told me to come back for dog before her husband came home and killed him. The other offered what appeared to

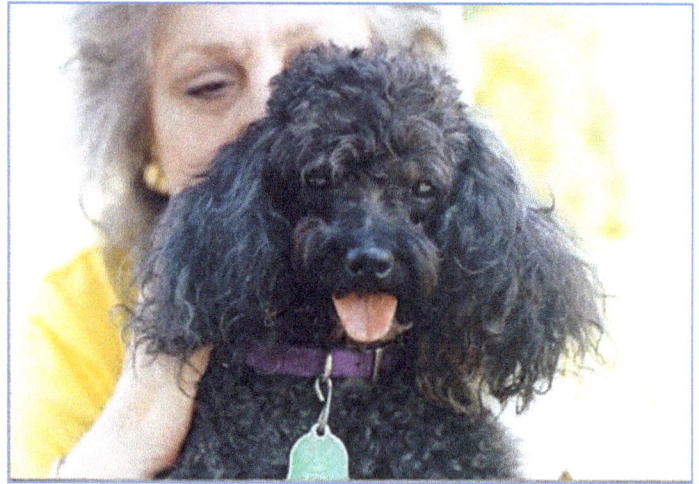

be a loving home, but as I was leaving, I heard the most yelping I had ever heard. I ran to see what was happening and found him already tied to a post with not enough lead to even sit down and two small children beating him up with sticks. The mother there said he had to get used to it as that was going to be his life! I reached into my pocket, bringing out her check, shredded it and said he will never get used to abuse, and I took him back home with me. I promised him I would find a way to keep him and love him forever.

One giant problem:-my husband Doug and I had only been married one year, and I didn't know how he would react to yet another dog in our home. So, I decided to have my daughter gift him to her new Dad knowing he would not turn our little black puppy away if our daughter had given him this puppy.

Yes, it was deceitful but I could not allow the puppy who was now known as Pierre to ever experience abuse again. It was my husband's birthday soon, and we had a birthday party for him. I kept Pierre on the bed during a scavenger hunt for Doug's gifts. The little dear was found at the end of many clues waiting quietly on the bed. Now I ask: who could not love a sweet eight week-old puppy with a birthday hat on his head when given to you from your daughter?

Yes, little Pierre was home to stay!

BOW WOW COOKIES

Ingredients:

- 2 cups Red Mill or organic rice flour
- 1 teaspoon baking powder
- 1 cup natural peanut butter
- 1 cup organic low fat milk
- 1 tablespoon agave
- 1 cup dried fruit (blueberries, strawberries, apples, bananas) diced small
- 1 chicken breast-cooked and ground-can combine two if you like

Directions:

Preheat to 350^0 F

In a large bowl combine all dry ingredients except fruit

Using a smaller bowl mix the milk, fruit, peanut butter, chicken and agave

Combine well

On a floured surface, knead and roll out to 1/4 inch thick. Using a cookie cutter, cut out your cookies

If too sticky add additional flour as needed

Place on a greased cookie sheet and bake for 18 to 20 minutes depending on your oven

Store in refrigerator in an air tight container

These cookies can be dried should you want a crispier drier cookie by following the dehydrator company instructions. If you have an oven that is capable of drying, that works almost as well.

Maggie Anne Goes Snap Snap!

by
Rosemary "Mamie" Adkins

It is role call time at Maggie's home. This is when her Mommie and Daddy take out her toy box and line up her playmates for the impending games. Now Maggie Anne gets to decide which ones she will pick out for her dinner games and dessert treats.

Mr. Greenie, Pickle, Rubie, Blackie, Mr. Football, Bone, Blue and all of Maggie's softer toys are gathered inside the playpen and toy box. Everyone is waiting for Maggie to decide who will share the fun with her.

Maggie knows dinner comes before she can have her special cookies but making up games to play while having dinner can also have its rewards. As she runs to Dad for her different toys she excitedly jumps up and down on the sofa's edge saying "snap snap." It hadn't taken us long to learn this meant she was ready for a big toss of one of the toys. She would chase after the toy and then dump it into Mommie's lap, trading it off for her dinner or a special treat, once dinner had finished.

Our little girl, while snapping her teeth, gives us the idea that she wants a gingerbread cookie as a treat, although at times she is simply wanting some affection. We have to pay close attention as Maggie has special games she plays, and she expects us to be listening and know what her special vocabulary is telling us!

Maggie has also become accustomed to our singing. Whatever the source of the music, it is quite comical and sweet to see her do her puppy dance as she shuffles her feet to the beat.

SNAP SNAP COOKIE

Ingredients:

- 1 ½ cups almond flour
- 2 tablespoons ginger, freshly grated
- 1 ½ teaspoons Ceylon cinnamon
- 1 ½ tablespoon organic agave (raw honey my be used if agave is not available
- ¾ cup filtered water or sugar free maple syrup
- ½ cup molasses
- 4 tablespoons extra virgin olive oil

Directions:

Preheat oven to 350⁰ F.

Combine all ingredients in a mixer or food processor.

Mix until a thick dough forms and roll out on a floured surface to 1/4 inch thick.

Cut out into desired shapes using your favorite cookie cutter.

Bake for 20 to 26 minutes depending on altitude and your oven.

HINT:

For crispier cookies you can either leave them in the oven after turning off until completely dried out (watch that they don't burn) or we use our dehydrator until dried out

Easy way for rolling out dough: Cut two lengths of parchment paper the same size and place the dough between them -flip the dough with paper in place and continue to roll dough evenly. Then slide rolled dough in parchment paper onto upside down cookie sheet and place in freezer for ten minutes so it firms up enough for easy quick cutting!

Chicky Chicken-Strips

Ingredients:

- 4 cups of chicken (5 chicken medium size breasts, boneless, skinless)
- 3 cups of sweet potatoes
- 1 ½ cups of oatmeal (use extra if recipe is too wet or runny)
- ⅛ cup molasses
- ⅛ cup of pure maple syrup
- ¼ teaspoon of saigon cinnamon
- 2 tablespoons olive oil
- ½ cup water

For Variation

Add 2 cups dried fruits that are allowable (See our section on Allowable foods for dogs)

1 teaspoon ground dried rosemary-we raise this herb and dry it. Then we use our herb grinder so we have fresh ground to use. It goes a long way so use sparingly.

Directions:

Boil or bake chicken until done adding a bit of Italian seasoning to the boiling water or on top of the chicken as it bakes. Once the chicken is done, allow it to cool before adding it in small sections to a food processor until all chicken is processed.

Add all ingredients except oatmeal

Once done, transfer to an electric mixer and add oatmeal mixing until dough is firm and not wet. If wet add additional dry oats.

We like to dehydrate the strip but it can be easily made into bite size cookies by placing 1/2 teaspoon on a cookie tray and making an impression with a fork across the centers and baking at 350 F until golden brown.

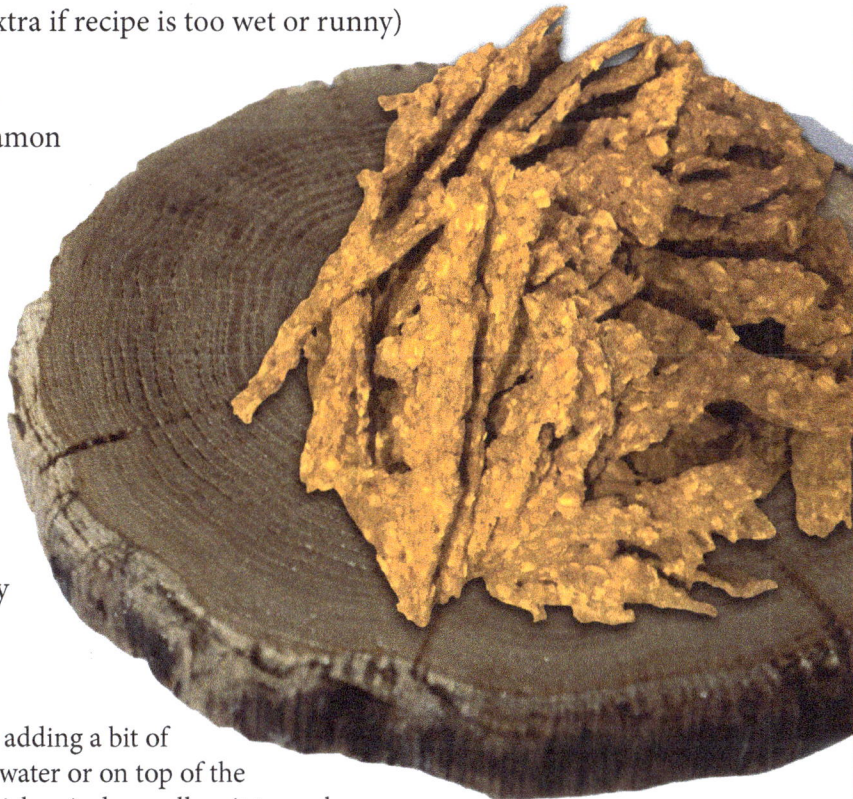

We found that the crunch is part of the attraction to this cookie. This is why we elected to dehydrate them, though we have baked them as well.

This recipe provides so many nutrients for your dog. We use only human grade ingredients and certainly recommend you use the best ingredients for the health of your dog.

Beneficial nutrition from this recipe: Protein from the chicken and the oats provide both protein and fiber, giving your dog a feeling of being full. Sweet potatoes provide Vitamins A and C as well as various B Vitamins.

DOUG'S CORNER

MAGGIE'S METHOD OF EATING HAS ALWAYS BEEN BEWILDERMENT TO ME. WE SPENT GOOD MONEY BUYING HER A FANCY FOOD & WATER BOWL BUT INSTEAD SHE WOULD RATHER EAT OFF THE FLOOR. I DECIDED TO PUT DOWN A COOKIE SHEET SO THAT THE FLOOR DIDN'T GET DIRTY ALL THE TIME. SHE DOESN'T LIKE TO EAT OUT OF THE BOWLS. SHE LOVES TO EAT THIS WAY. GO FIGURE. WE ALSO HAVE BOUGHT HER LOTS OF TOYS TO ENTERTAIN HER AND KEEP HER MIND OCCUPIED. WHAT SHE ENJOYS THE MOST THOUGH, ARE EMPTY 1/2 GALLON PLASTIC JUICE BOTTLES OR EMPTY GALLON MILK JUGS. SHE THEN CHASES THEM AROUND THE KITCHEN - MAKES LOTS OF NOISE. WHEN SHE WAS A BABY THE BOTTLES WOULD LAST SEVERAL HOURS. AS SHE GOT OLDER, THEY DIDN'T LAST LONG AT ALL BEFORE SHE DESTROYED THEM. THE TIME DID COME WHEN WE HAD TO STOP GIVING THEM TO HER. TOO BAD!

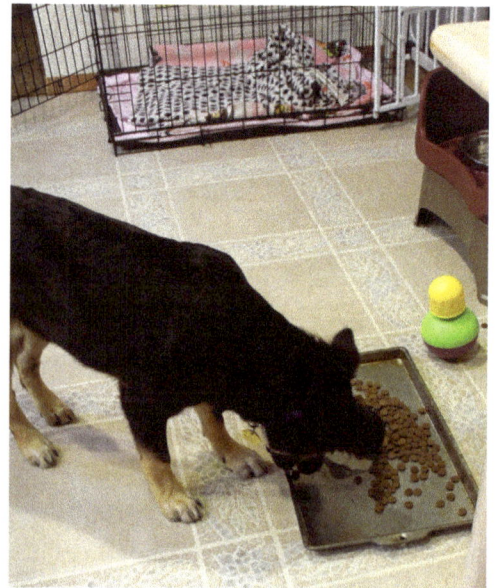

Pup Pup Chews

Puppies are known to chew everything from rawhides to that forbidden treasure belonging to their human parent. Instead of frustrations for everyone, why not provide them with a delicious chewy chicken treat packed full of protein satisfying that craving they think they are getting from your best pair of shoes!

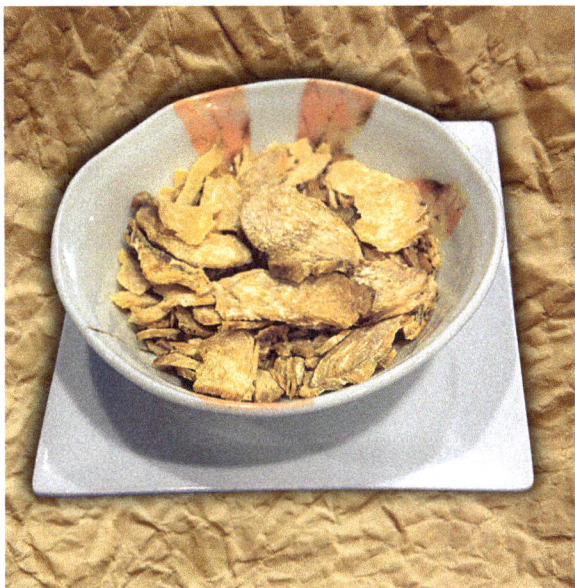

Ingredients

- 3 chicken breasts
- 2 tablespoons extra virgin olive oil
- 1 teaspoon Italian seasoning

OPTION:

Drizzle (very small amount of pure maple syrup across the chicken strips while mixing the ingredients or sprinkle very lightly a bit of cinnamon

Directions

Preheat oven to 200-225^{0}F or follow manufacturer's guide in a food dehydrator.

Rinse all chicken breasts and pat dry, then slice into very thin strips. Be sure to have trimmed all fat and skin from the chicken breast prior to slicing.

Place the strips into a medium size bowl and add all ingredients, mixing well. Then, if drying in the oven, place slices on a cookie sheet being careful not to allow pieces to touch. If using a dehydrator place on the liner of the drying tray also not touching one piece to another.

Bake at low temperature for 2 hours or until done (should dry snap when cooled) We like to dehydrate as they seem to make a crispier treat

Cool completely before storing in an air tight container in the refrigerator.

Chews are great for training treats or that special reward treat.

These will keep for up to two (2) weeks.

Hint:

If you freeze the chicken breast for about 30 minutes, slicing is much easier.

Substitutes:

You can use this process for drying fruit and vegetables for a chewy treat. Apricots or sweet potatoes are great substitutes using the same seasonings.

Bananza Banana Chips

One day I decided to make Momo some banana treats with even more bananas added into the recipe than in the banana pancakes we had been making her. I wanted to try to make them taste even more like a banana. However, instead of a pancake texture, I ended up with a texture I thought could be made into a yummy chip. Now, these have become Momo's all-time favorites that we like to take with us as rewards on her walks. They store very well in your pocket and do not crumble, but they will break up easily in small bite-size pieces when you need to divide them for treats on your walks.

Banana chips are ready for the oven

Ingredients:
- 1 cup mashed banana
- 1 tablespoon unsulphured Blackstrap Molasses
- 1 tablespoon water
- 1 tablespoon olive oil
- ¼ cup whole wheat flour (or quinoa flour)
- ¼ cup whole rolled oat flour
- 1 teaspoon flaxseed meal

Directions:
Preheat oven to 350^{0}F.

Mix banana, molasses, water, and olive oil together in a medium size mixing bowl.

Add the flours and flaxseed meal and mix together (use hands to knead dough).

With lightly wet hands, scoop a tablespoon into your hands and roll in a ball (half as much for small dogs).

Place the ball onto a lightly greased cookie and be sure and use wet hands to smash the batter on the cooking sheet to become flattened to ⅛ in or less and make into the shape of a chip. These only need 20 minutes to cook and make about 3 dozen.

Hot banana chips cooked for a delicious and healthy treat to take on your walks!

Maggie Loves De'Feet

by
Rosemary "Mamie" Adkins

OMG this dog is so smart! Here she is having the last laugh as she rolls in the grass thinking she had won at her new game!

Maggie is certainly a chewer. Biting my feet was her worst habit. Correct that: my worst mistake was teaching her what I thought would be a fun game When she arrived she came with a ton of energy. So in self-defense and for the purpose of using up at least some of her energy, I decided it would be exciting to pretend to chase her around our center kitchen island. Now, when we adopted her she was full of fear (it turned out a woman was the abuser and the feet played a huge role), but I did not know that at the time. I only hoped this silly game would indeed burn some energy and get her to channel the biting elsewhere then at my feet.

NEVER START what you don't want to do every day of your life! I stomped my feet and she ran around and around and around over and over again. Our heads spun with dizziness watching her work so hard while we just stood in one spot. The next morning after she had gone potty, she pranced into the kitchen where I was making my coffee at this same island. Maggie wanted to play so she promptly came to me and bit my feet, then took off to run around the island! Each time around she bit my feet to get me started—WHAT HAD I DONE??

Four weeks later I was still putting on boots and spraying them with a solution that Maggie doesn't like in order to enter the kitchen without having my feet attacked! Maggie is so smart and she wouldn't forget the game, thinking this is how it should start—my feet moving around to play with her (even if she had to bite me to make that happen)! In self-defense, I reached for another homemade treat and to my delight it stopped her from thinking the d'feet were the tastiest. The treat I used was one of Maggie's original treats! The Chezzpaw Cookies!

A prisoner in our own home, I now have gates across the area where the coffee pot is located so if she comes in from her morning potty break before my coffee is made, I'm safe! That's our Maggie!

DOUG'S CORNER

WE WERE BARBECUING ON THE CHARCOAL BBQ ONE NIGHT. MAMIE LIKES TO DO MARSHMALLOWS ON THE COALS. MAGGIE WAS TRYING TO GET SOME TREATS FROM HER. SHE GOT A FEW PIECES BUT NOT MUCH. ALMOST LIKE AROUND THE CAMPFIRE - BUT WHEN SHE IS DONE SHE GETS TO GO IN THE HOUSE INSTEAD OF HAVING TO SLEEP IN A SLEEPING BAG. FEELING HAPPY.

The Chezzpaw Cookies!

Maggie Approved

Ingredients:
- 1 ½ cups white rice flour. See notes below about other flours used.
- 1 ¼ cups grated cheddar cheese.
- 3 ½ ounces butter
- Milk–you may need a small amount to help form the dough. I use canned evaporated milk.

Directions:

Turn oven on at 325^0F.

Use a non stick cookie sheet or Pam on a regular cookie sheet. We like the olive oil cooking spray for added mild flavor.

Leave the grated cheese on the counter until it is room temperature. You can use a pre-grated mix of cheeses for variety.

Using a fork, blend the cheese and butter together until it is creamed.

Add rice flour or an oat flour (Sometimes I double this recipe and add both rice flour and oat flour using 1-1/2 cups of each or split the recipe using 3/4 cup of each flour, giving you a texture change).

Add some milk if needed and knead until it forms a ball.

Chill for 30 minutes.

Roll out on floured surface until about 1/2 inch thick.

Use your knife or cookie cutter to make shapes.

Place on a non-stick baking tray and put into the oven for 30 minutes. Ovens and altitude make a difference, so after 20 minutes you may want to begin checking for the time that works best for your area and oven.

Leave to cool before storing.

NOTE: If you double this recipe, you will have a lot of cookies to share. It is especially fun to cut them out in bone, hydrant or dog house shapes with your cookie cutters.

Sleeping Angel with a Saving Voice
by
Rosemary "Mamie" Adkins

Now here is an interesting story, and we would like to share it with you. Some time ago I was home alone with our puppy Maggie (getting ready for physical therapy) while Doug was running errands. Maggie started barking and would not stop. This was not like her, so I kept looking for a reason and found nothing. I returned to the back of the house to finish getting ready, but Maggie would not stop barking—and it got worse.

Soon after Maggie came to me and looked at me with a strange stare while barking, I told her I had not seen what was wrong and told her to settle down. She was very nervous, but I continued to get ready.

It was then that Doug came home. Maggie ran down the hall to the door, barking like crazy. Doug yelled out to me, "I think we are on fire! Get out here."

I ran with one shoe on and the other falling off to see thick smoke with a strange odor filling the hallway and front of the house. Doug was able to determine it was a faulty light bulb in the ceiling which was hot and had turned black.

Luckily a fire had been averted. Maggie had tried so hard to make me listen. I'm so sorry sweet girl–you saved our lives again!

We all left the house together, and while I was at physical therapy Doug and Maggie went for a long walk so she could relax after such a traumatic beginning for the day.

Though she had been up for this walk, she still seemed worked up and troubled. So, onward to another adventure for her in hopes of having some fun.

We had seen she displayed an interest in water while getting wet over the last several weeks, and we knew there was a creek was nearby. That's all it took for Miss Maggie Anne! Oh, how she loves the water! She dove into the creek and washed away all her troubles. It also appeared she had seen something in the water that had her attention, and she was set on catching it.

Could it be while she was paddling in the creek that the little something she was chasing under the water was a fish? Well, now we had a new idea for a treat for our Maggie other than chicken. Something fishy

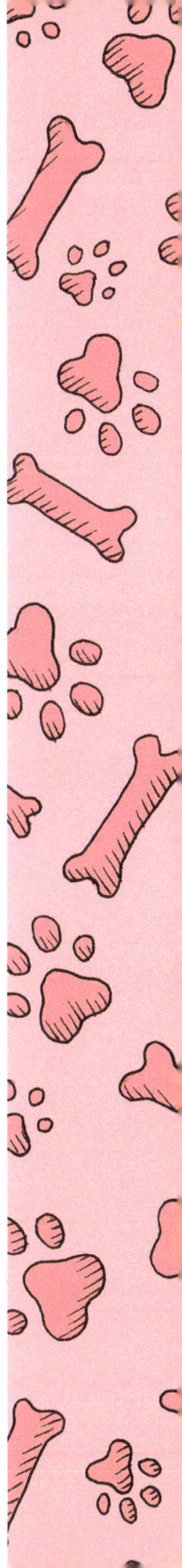

Passed out from her busy day, Maggie was our sleeping angel. She was exhausted from this ordeal, our little hero. Now who couldn't love a sweet baby like this. That was our lucky day.

Doug's Corner

RECENTLY WE HAVE BEEN REALLY BUSY AROUND THE HOUSE DOING SOME SPRING CLEANING AND HAD NOT HAD MUCH TIME TO "ENTERTAIN/PLAY" WITH MAGGIE. YESTERDAY I WAS AT A PHYSICAL THERAPY APPOINTMENT AND MAMIE WAS BUSY IN THE KITCHEN. MAGGIE DECIDED SHE WAS BORED SO SHE FOUND THE ROLL OF TOILET PAPER IN MY BATHROOM (UP TO NOW SHE HAS LEFT IT ALONE). THE PICTURE TO THE RIGHT SHOWS WHAT WAS LEFT OF IT.

THE PICTURE TO THE LEFT SHOWS YOU WHAT SHE REALLY ENJOYS DOING - CHASING HER BALL.

Fishy Fishy Fishy!

This is a favorite of so many.

Ingredients:

- 16 ounces total of albacore tuna, crab and salmon
- 1 ½ cups brown rice flour
- 4 ounces salmon cream cheese
- ¼ teaspoon Italian seasoning
- ⅛ teaspoon garlic (See notes for kind we use)
- Pinch of salt

Directions:

Preheat oven to 350⁰F.

Using a cookie sheet, prepare with olive oil cooking spray or a cake pan size 8 x 8 or 13 x 9. The first time I made this, I used the cake pan and it worked great but it was a thick cookie. I recommend you use a cookie sheet for an easy to break apart treat. Either way is fine.

Combine the fish using the liquid and break it apart mixing the three types and add the flour blending well in a mixer.

In food processor combine all ingredients. It WILL be sticky.

Remove and pour into pan. It will be sticky and thick but spread it to all corners of the pan with a spatula.

Bake for 40 minutes, if using a cake pan but check it after 30 minutes for varying ovens. In a cookie sheet, bake until crisp, about 15 to 20 minutes.

For added crispness, I like to add it to the food dehydrator and cook it overnight. This treat should be refrigerated or frozen to maintain its goodness.

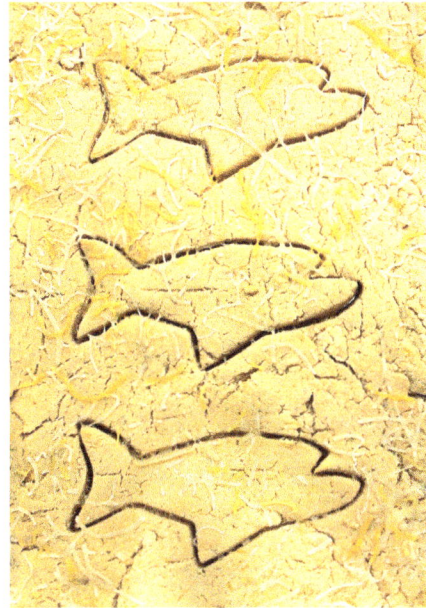

Missin' Maggie Anne Oatmeal Cookies

Ingredients:

- ¾ cup dry oats
- 1 ½ cups oat flour
- 1 ½ cups rice flour
- 1 tablespoon vanilla
- 1 teaspoon cinnamon
- ½ cup melted butter
- 2 eggs
- ¼ cup maple syrup
- ¼ cup apple sauce
- ¾ cup carob chips-*optional*

Directions:

Pre Heat Oven to 350⁰ F.

Coat cookie sheet with cooking spray.

Mix dry ingredients until well blended-except carob.

Add vanilla, butter, syrup, eggs, water, and apple sauce.

Blend well.

Fold in carob chips.

Use your favorite cookie cutters or drop cookies put the cookies on the cookie sheet.

Bake for 20 to 25 minutes or until golden brown.

After baking, dehydrate cookies overnight to achieve longer storage and a crispier texture.

Yields approximately 50 flat 2" cookies.

HINT: If your dog does not like carob, then it is recommended that this ingredient be left out of the recipe.

HOOTIN N' HOWLIN BEEF STICKS

Ingredients:

- 2 cups white rice
- 1 ½ cups vermicelli-broken in pieces ¼ inch in length
- 6 cups filtered water
- 2 tablespoons butter
- 3 pounds of lean ground beef
- 1 ½ cups dry oats (we use Quaker)

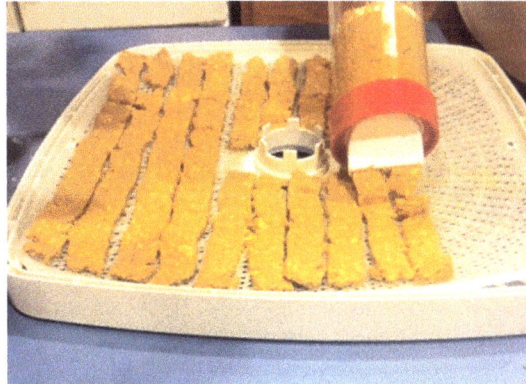

Directions:

In a rice cooker, place the 2 cups of rice and 6 cups of water.

On your stove top heat butter in a skillet and be careful not to burn it. Then add the vermicelli and cook until browned. DO NOT TURN YOUR BACK on this one or it will burn!

After browned, turn off the heat and add 1/4 cup of water and cover the skillet to steam the vermicelli for two minutes.

Add vermicelli to the rice cooker and follow your rice cooker instructions for rice.

While the rice is cooking, brown 3 pounds of the leanest ground beef you can find. We look for 7% fat or less. It makes a drier jerky and is better for your dogs. Use a meat grinder or similar product and grind the meat very fine.

Now using a food processor, blend together the meat and rice. Once blended, remove from food processor and move to your stand mixer and add the oats. There is too much mixture to try to do this all in most food processors.

After the oats are well blended, you can either bake as cookies or dehydrate them. When dehydrating we use a jerky gun for even strips. If as a cookie, drop mixture by the teaspoon and flattened to 1/4 inch thick and bake at 350⁰F until done. Except for the oats this is already cooked so watch as not to burn them.

Follow the dehydrator instructions for beef jerky. Check for doneness when no moisture is present and it snaps when you break it.

Using the same ingredients and fat content on beef, we had 2 ½ pounds of jerky after dehydrating which is enough to last for a few weeks so be sure to freeze what cannot be used in 3 days. SAFETY ALWAYS FIRST PLEASE!

This is great treat for training, long walks or those times when that special treat is needed.

Lucky Dog Okanawan Sweet Potato Delights

Momo will also do her many tricks for these Okanawan, sweet potato and wild salmon delights and loves them almost as much as banana treats.

Ingredients:

- ¼ cup mashed, cooked, Okanawan sweet potoates (peeled)*
- ½ teaspoon olive oil
- ½ cup wild Alaskan salmon (if in can be sure it is boneless and skinless, drain water and rinse well if salt has been added)
- 1 tablespoon filtered water
- ⅓ cup whole oats flour (I grind oats in a coffee grinder)
- 1 teaspoon flaxseed meal
- ⅛ teaspoon baking soda
- ⅛ teaspoon baking powder

*You can also use cooked, mashed carrots as a substitute for sweet potatoes.

Directions:

Preheat oven to 350^0F.

Mix sweet potatoes, olive oil, salmon and filtered water together.

Add the flour and mix together. Then add flaxseed meal, baking soda, and baking powder to the mixture and knead until mixed completely and the dough softens.

The oat flour should make it easy to smash out on a floured surface, and use a cookie cutter to make shapes. Bake about 20 minutes, until dough is slightly hardened. Remember that it will cook and harden after you have taken it out of the oven. Let them cool before serving.

Okanawan sweet potato and wild salmon treats.

Maggie Waits for Her Cookie

by
Rosemary "Mamie" Adkins

She waits. And she waits some more. Finally, Maggie sees herself in the oven door but finds something even more exciting—her very own cookie idea being baked before her eyes.

Now, Maggie has given her approval to these. I got the hint when she so enjoyed the marinara sauce we made for dinner.

She sat patiently by the stove, quietly sniffing, as if to say "Please share that with me." And of course, her little face with those adoring eyes just spoke to us, so we gave in by dipping a small cheese cookie (hers) into some marinara sauce. She loved them. And what can I say? A new recipe was soon created!

Our recipes are seldom made with the use of wheat or white flours, because we try to stay wheat free with

MAGGIE sits and waits for her treats

treats. But you are welcome to substitute the flour of your choosing. We enjoy Bob's Red Mill Flours for the quality they provide. We also use filtered water and organic ingredients. So, if possible, please consider that what you put into these treats are for the overall health of your family pet.

I cannot tell you the exact quantity as I use many sizes for variation but you should get about 75 cookies.

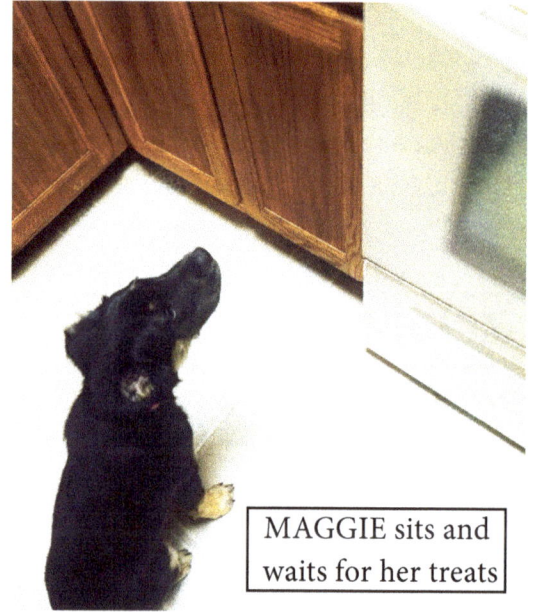

Cheesy Hearts Afire Tomato Basil Angel Cookie

Ingredients:

- 2 cups rice, rye, oat flour or other non grain flour (You can use a white or wheat flour but we always use the above or Gluten free flour)
- ⅓ cup milk
- 1 egg
- 3 tablespoons butter
- 1 can tomato paste (6 ounces)
- ½ cup shredded mozzarella or provolone cheese
- 1 teaspoon cinnamon
- 1 teaspoon raw sugar
- 2 teaspoons dried basil
- 1 teaspoon oregano
- 1 teaspoon rosemary

OPTIONS: To aid the digestion, we sometimes add 1 teaspoon of parsley

Directions:

Preheat oven to 350^0F.

In a mixer bowl, blend everything together until mixed well. Scoop the dough out onto a work surface dusted with a little extra flour.

Knead dough into ball. If the dough gets too sticky, add a little extra flour, a small amount at a time to avoid it becoming too dry.

Roll the dough out to approximately 1/4 inch thickness (if wanting a crispy cookie, we roll out to 1/8 inch in thickness) and cut out shapes with a cookie cutter. We have fun using shapes like bones, fire hydrants, dog houses and paws.

Use a well greased cookie sheet (cooking spray) or parchment paper and your cookies are now ready for the oven. Bake for 10 minutes. or until golden brown.

Cool on a wire racks.

These MUST be kept these in the refrigerator to protect keep them from spoiling. For safety, you may want to consider freezing in an airtight container what can't be enjoyed inside one week.

NOTE: Substitutions can also be used.

We have also made these with fresh tomatoes, diced very small.

Maggie Saves the Day!
by
Rosemary "Mamie" Adkins

This heartwarming story took place on a beautiful sunny day. The rays were shining brightly through our kitchen bay window, and I felt energized to do something special for my sweet Maggie Anne! I decided to test my new cookie idea to see how she liked it. After all, it contained her most favorite thing-sweet potatoes! I was pretty sure that this was definitely one for our new *Maggie's Kitchen Tails* cookbook! What a great way to reward her for loving us back as much as we love her.

I have over the years found a routine of checks and balances when baking or beginning a project, so I gather what is needed before I begin.

Okay then, let's get started! Ingredients … check! Utensils … check. Food processor … Aw shucks! I forgot to have Doug get it out for me. Well, that was not going to hamper my excitement today. I bent down to remove my processor from a lower shelf, and as I attempted to stand up I lost my balance and fell flat on my back onto the kitchen floor! I managed to get into a sitting position but, try as I might, I was simply unable to stand up.

Maggie was in the front room sitting on her bench chewing on a bone and must have heard the sound of my fall. Startled, she made a beeline to my side, sounding for all the world, like a stampede of wild horses. She sat beside me as I was having a good cry, and I could see the wheels turning in her mind-how can I help my Mommy?

I had to think this through very carefully. First, I was able to reach for my cell phone on the kitchen counter and proceeded to call my husband several times to no avail. Normally he picks up but, just my luck, not this time. The neuropathy in my legs due to diabetes made it even more difficult, and I began to fear that I would be stuck on the floor until he came home. To make matters even worse, I have one knee that won't bend. What a sorry mess I was in.

So there we were, just Maggie and me! Maggie knew that I was having trouble and was trying to comfort me. As I repeatedly made the effort to pull myself up, she gently lapped up my tears and tried to reassure me with her gentle kisses. Clearly beside herself with worry, Maggie kept stepping back, reassessing the situation and returning to kiss away my tears.

I suddenly had the idea that if I could scoot my way over to the chair against the wall, I'd be able to pull myself up to sit on it. I reached the chair just fine, but with every attempt to rise I kept falling back down again. I could see that Maggie was getting agitated and wanted so desperately to help. She knew I was in trouble, so perhaps her classes in becoming a service dog have come in handy. She had already proven herself by waking me on a couple of occasions when my blood sugar was extremely low and needed attention. No, she knew that this was serious and not our usual playtime.

And then it happened! Without warning, Maggie rushed to my side to do her part. She braced her head and shoulders firmly between my legs and pushed with all of her might, giving me the leverage I needed to get up onto the chair. She saved the day!

This little girl was barely one year old, yet she had the intelligence and focus to come up with a plan on her own to save me. Maggie Anne is definitely my hero and acts more like a well-trained service dog every day. More than ever, Maggie deserved those cookies that I was in the process of baking for her and after a rest she was going to have them. The angel markings on her chest say it all for us. I love our sweet girl so much!

She is my hero and certainly deserves these cookies along with a million kisses. How can a puppy just barely one year old be so strong and so very smart? No one had better ever question that she is my Service Dog … in training or otherwise. I love her dearly!

Sweet Potato Crunchie

Ingredients:
- 1 cup oats
- 1 cup cooked sweet potatoes*
- ⅓ cup smooth peanut butter
- ½ cup oat flour
- 2 teaspoons molasses
- Dash of cinnamon

Directions:

Sweet Potatoes-peel and cut into chucks for boiling (3 medium size organic sweet potatoes).

Cook until done and mash with 1 tablespoon molasses.

Measure out 1 cup and add to the oats, flour and peanut butter. Add a dash of cinnamon and add molasses.

Add the other ingredients together and blend well.

Using a teaspoon take out the batter and roll into a ball. Make an impression on top of the cookie and bake!

Bake: Preheat to 350^0 F. Bake for 20 to 25 minutes.

Twist and Bark Mozzarella Treats!

Ingredients:

- 1 ¾ cups oat flour
- ¼ cup rice flour
- ¼ cup corn meal
- ⅛ teaspoon sea salt
- ¾ cup grated cheese-most any kind like romano, split half
- 2 tablespoons tomato paste
- 2 eggs, beaten with ¾ cup water
- ¼ teaspoon Italian seasoning
- ¼ teaspoon ground rosemary

Directions:

Preheat the oven to 325⁰ F.

In a large bowl, mix together the flours, corn meal, salt, and half of the cheese and Italian Seasoning. Add the whipped eggs and water. Mix until it forms soft dough. The dough may feel sticky so you may need to add additional flour to it. On a floured surface, knead well. Using a rolling pin, roll the dough to ½ inch thickness.

Spread the left over cheese on the prepared dough and place a sheet of parchment paper on top and roll again so that it embeds into the dough at the surface. It helps give the twist a crunchier texture.

Cut 1/2 wide inch strips length wise and then 6 inches long. Twist each strip like a twisted donut and place on a cookie sheet, well-greased or lined with parchment paper. Bake for 20 to 25 minutes or until they begin to brown.

Store in the refrigerator in an airtight container or freeze what you can't use in a week.

*OPTION: At this stage, for a longer lasting treat use a food dehydrator and dry until they are done making them crispy.

A CHILD'S BEST FRIENDS
DUCK AND A DOG?
by
Rosemary "Mamie" Adkins

Way back in time (please do not ask how far back!) my family lived in a small suburb of Houston, Texas in an area just being developed with new homes that backed up to an easement that kept us private for some distance. It was the perfect place to have animals but no one expected we would have this beautiful white soft feathery bird with a bright yellow bill. This creature loved living in the back of the house where it could eat the bugs and swim all day. Her best friend was also a surprise to the neighborhood as she was like no other four legged canine they had ever seen before and certainly not like a "normal dog".

You may be asking about now what was so different with these animals, so I will tell you it was because the white fluffy bird was a duck. In Houston? She and our dog loved to play. Our dog's name was Miss Daisy and the duck's name was Nuisance—which she earned on her own! Our dog was said to be a bird hunting dog and the duck? Under normal circumstances it would have been Miss Daisy's lunch! But they were both misfits and very close friends.

Nuisance came with another name of Sweetie but soon after she took up residence with us and became my pet, her name was changed. Here is how that happened …

Tic toc tic toc. It's 5 AM and the alarm is suddenly sounding. No, not the traditional alarm clock, but the DUCK alarm. Mother shouts out and says to me: *"Get up and go take care of Sweetie before the neighbors call the police."* I was eight years old and loved that duck, but soon her name changed to Nuisance! What a fitting name, yes? Every day it was the same thing. She wanted me to come outside in my PJ's and slippers accompanied by Miss Daisy and her breakfast. It was the hour I objected to, but in time I did not need to hear a voice telling me to get up, as it was Miss Daisy who would wake me so we could go out to see Nuisance.

Those two became my whole world filled with love from them (but endless loads of chores were connected to them as well). One of these chores was to find them when they decided to take their stroll in the wee hours of a day. This was most inconvenient on school mornings, because I would be so tired by school time that I would get into trouble for falling asleep at my desk. They always took their walks after sharing a dip in the pond my father had dug out for Nuisance. She swam and Miss Daisy put her front feet into the pond, splashing about, making a mess and, of course, lots of noise.

Nuisance and Miss Daisy would take their walks before breakfast and could be found sitting at a different neighbor's door each morning as if waiting for an invitation to dine. They were good at walking and it was not long before they decided to follow me to school each day and return about an hour before school let out so they could explore. They found their new playground most interesting and food the kids would leave outside was a real treasure. I was popular that school year as no one could believe that two very different animals could be best friends. And the fact that they loved me enough to waddle their way all the way twice each day? Wow! Just imagine a bird hunting dog and a duck. It was not long before my world was filled with friends, walking down the neighborhood street like they were being led by the Pied Piper. Two very different pets, we but we were all one big happy family.

Sometimes when thinking back I wonder why those two loved one another so much or why they teamed up with me. Maybe we were all three alike in some way. I'm not sure, but I know I loved them with my whole heart, and I felt so important knowing they did care so much.

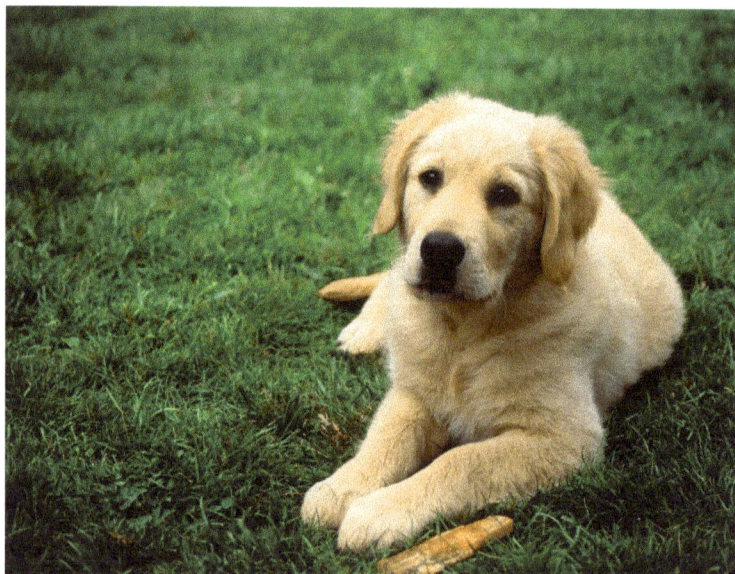

CRAN-PUMPKIN DOG COOKIES

Ingredients:

- 2 ½ cups gluten free flour
- 2 tablespoons flax meal*
- 1 extra large egg, lightly beaten
- 1 cup fresh cranberries **
- 1 cup canned pumpkin puree (not the spiced kind used for pies)
- 1 teaspoon baking soda
- 2 teaspoons baking powder

OPTION:

1/4 cup cold water or enough to make the dough bind if needed

Directions:

Preheat oven to 350^0 F.

Line two baking sheets with parchment paper.

Combine flour and flax meal in a large bowl.

Whip egg and pumpkin together in a separate bowl until smooth.

Add half of the pumpkin mixture to the flour mixture.

Mix well and then add the remaining ingredients and blend with a spatula.

Add water slowly, as needed.

Using your hands knead the dough

Roll dough out between two pieces of parchment paper to desired thickness, no more than 1/4" thick.

Place the parchment paper with dough between it in the freezer for ten minutes-this is optional but makes cutting easier.

Remove top parchment paper, flipping the dough onto a floured counter .

Remove the last piece of parchment paper and using your favorite cookie cutters, cut out the dough until used completely reshaping scraps each time.

Bake:

Place cut out cookies on parchment lined baking sheets (or sheets lightly greased with oil).

Bake for 30 to 45 minutes until the cookie tops have dried out completely.

Remove from oven and cool on wire racks.

Store in an airtight container.

This recipe will make approximately 36 large bone cut outs. We like to make smaller cookies for reward cookies so we make half large and half smaller giving us approximately 54 cookies. This count is based on the cookie cutter used.

*If you have whole flax seed-just grind into a powder

**cranberries need to be lightly cooked or use canned whole berry cranberry sauce

This recipe should yield about 65 cookies, using a 3" dog bone cookie cutter.

Magic and Elfie

by
Martha Char Love
Magic and Elfie, mother and son

We can attest that rescued dogs can make fantastic mother dogs. Our dog, Magic, who was rescued as a puppy, had a litter of 8 puppies to which Elfie was born. Due to her early abuse before she came to our family, Magic was a bit nervous (often barking at things that were not there and hoarding food), but she loved her son Elfie and he was never alone or separated from her, which had a profound positive affect upon his emotional and intellectual state. He was a King of a dog. This was in great part because he had such a loving mother as Magic and in part because he was just born an outstanding being.

Magic Munches Apples

Magic was a German Shepherd-St Bernard mix that we rescued as a four week old puppy from a box of eight to ten puppies being given away in front of our local Safeway grocery store. I say rescued because the human being giving the puppies away said she was on her way to the pound to dump them off. Magic was the runt of the litter, squeaking down in the bottom of the box. We pulled her out from under the pile of wiggling fur balls, cuddled her in our arms, told her we loved her and that we were taking her home. Most babies of mammal species stop crying when you pick them up, feed them, and love them. But Magic did not stop crying for nearly 48 hours, even though we were cuddling her day and night. Finally, we managed to have her feel safe and she began to show signs of happiness.

She had to be the funniest dog we have ever had and she kept our family laughing at the crazy things she would do, like making honking goose-like sounds when she was happy and chasing after things that were just not there (at least we couldn't see them, but maybe she was a ghost buster). When Magic was inside the house, she spent 90 percent of her time guarding her food bowl from our other dog (who was also her own son), Elfie, so that he would never get to eat any of "her" food, which he truly never cared about anyway.

Our country house in Northern California had a small apple orchid in the back and Magic could often be found eating an apple that had fallen from the trees. She somehow knew to not eat the poisonous seeds or stems. Apples are a healthy treat for dogs as they contain calcium, vitamin K, vitamin C, and pectin (which is a soluble fiber). Apples can be served like other treats as a fresh slice in a Kong (no seeds or stems), or for hot weather you can make apple pops for your dog using apple sauce in an ice tray.

One year, I decided to dehydrate some apple slices for Magic for the winter months when the apples would disappear from our yard. I didn't have a dehydrator, so I cut up the pieces and placed them in a new pair of panty hose and tied the end to secure them from falling out. Then I hung the apples in the hose up in our kitchen from a hanging basket attached to the ceiling. This way, ants could not get to them. And, yes, it did look a little funny! After a couple of weeks, the apple slices would dry naturally. I'm not sure this would work in a colder climate, and I always did this at the end of the summer when it was still warm and dry outside, with plenty of ripe apples to gather.

Of course, you do not have to use hose to dry your apples because you can dehydrate apples in your dehydrator. Now, since dried apples have very little water content, be sure and only feed very small amounts of them to your dog so it does not get an upset stomach. And of course, fresh apples are the best because dogs can eat much more of the fresh ones! Magic loved these dried apples, and I could even get her to come away from guarding her food bowl to eat a piece of a dried apple treat!

Magic's Honking Good Apple Munchies

Here is another munchable treat-using apples and pumpkin-that I have made for the dogs in my life today. But if my Magic dog were still with me, I know she would love eating them and would give one of her famous "honks" for happiness, so I have named this recipe for her.

Ingredients:

- 1 cup cooked pumpkin (from a can is fine if it is pure organic pumpkin and can has BPA free liner)
- ¼ teaspoon olive oil or coconut oil
- 1 tablespoon black strap molasses
- ½ cup buckwheat flour
- ¾ cup oat flour
- ⅛ teaspoon baking soda
- ⅛ teaspoon baking powder
- 1 Granny Smith apple, cored and grated (about 1 cup)
- ½ teaspoon cinnamon (optional, remember that most cinnamon bought in the USA is kin to the pea and not true cinnamon)

Directions:

Preheat oven to 325^0F. Combine pumpkin, oil, and molasses. Add flours to pumpkin mixture, and then add baking powder and baking soda, stir, and then add apples and cinnamon.

Knead dough until well mixed and stays held together.

Divide dough in two parts. With lightly wet hands, scoop a tablespoon into your hands and roll into a ball.

Place the ball onto a lightly greased cookie sheet and press the ball down to flatten, only ⅛ to ¼ inch in height.

Bake about 30 minutes.

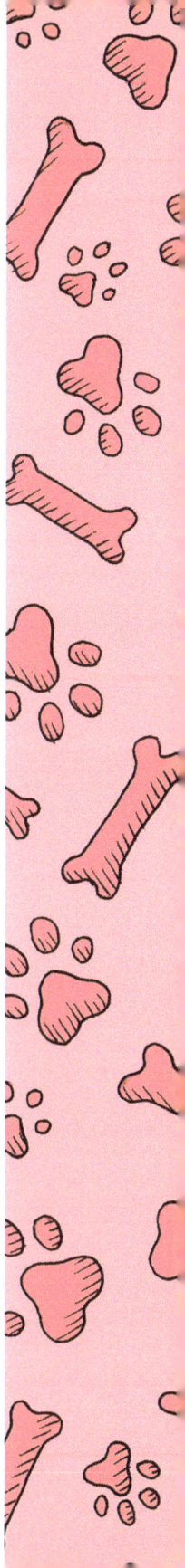

While the first batch is cooking, prepare the second half of the dough and place on a second cookie baking sheet. Cook second batch while first batch cools.

Store in airtight container in refrigerator or freezer bags in freezer.

DOUG'S CORNER

Today while Mamie was in a medical appointment I took Maggie out to "do her thing". It was very cold today and the wind was blowing pretty hard. After I bent over to pick up her deposit (like a good dog owner) & I was tying the bag shut - my hat blew off down the street. I took out after one of my favorite hats as it blew down the street with a bag of poo in one hand and Maggie trying to trip me with the leash in the other. I thought the worse but it ended up just fine as I caught my hat, with a car having to stop from running us both over, and managed to get out of the street with dog on one hand and poo bag in the other. All worked out just fine.

ANGELS IN FLIGHT
by
Rosemary "Mamie" Adkins

I believe in angels, don't you?

It was a Friday evening as we sat around the dinner table when my husband and I discovered we really do have an angel in our home and she is quite capable of flight!

Well, ok maybe not flight they way you may be thinking but she took us quite by surprise.

We had been having dinner while Maggie Anne was gnawing away on her bone in the dining room that I began to choke. The week prior to this evening, I had had major surgery on my spinal cord with several fusions so I was not on my best game but little did I know that was not the case for our angel, Maggie Anne.

The choking became severe and I began retching while Maggie became agitated and my choking grew as desperate as she was.

Maggie Anne

Before I knew it, she had flown into my lap trying to lick my face and acted as though she wanted to breathe for me. Doug standing behind me slapped my back forcing up what had lodged in my throat! Little Miss Maggie Anne tried to save the day again and was not all that crazy about Doug slapping my back. It's a good thing she loves us both so much.

So yes, we have both an angel in our home, an angel that can fly!

Next time you see this face walking down the street, be sure you wave.

This special cookie treat is just for you Maggie and all your friends!

Apple-Carrot Cookie Tango

Ingredients:

- 3 cups flax and gluten free flour
- 1 cup dry Quaker oats-They are inexpensive and add vitamin B, iron, zinc, fiber and they are high in protein to list a few reasons we like to use oats in most all of our dogs treats.
- ½ cup grated organic carrots-be sure you pat them dry of excess liquid
- ½ cup organic apples peeled and diced \ (1/2 medium apple)
- ½ mango-diced-drain off any liquid in a strainer-fresh organic is healthier. If unable to find, used canned mango's (15oz-light syrup) using about ½ the can. Save about 4 tablespoons of the syrup.
- ½ teaspoon of cinnamon-we recommend Ceylon cinnamon-beware, it is expensive but worth it.
- 1 teaspoon olive oil
- ⅓ cup pure maple syrup
- 2 tablespoons molasses
- ½ cup apple juice or water (and have extra on hand in case needed)

Have additional rice flour for rolling, about one cup

Directions:

Preheat oven to 350° F

Mix dry ingredients together.

Then in separate bowl mix: carrots, apples and mangos-where possible use organic fresh fruits.

Combine flour mixture and fruit

Add oil, syrup and molasses to combined mixture

If batter is too dry add more apple juice (sparingly or hot water adding only 1/8 cup at a time depending on the thickness). **Do not buy apple juice with added sugar**

The dough may be too sticky-if so, add additional flour

Knead the dough well. Form into a ball and wrap with plastic wrap and refrigerate for 10 minutes .

Roll out the dough into 1/8" or 1/4" thickness and using your doggie cookie cutters cut into shapes. You may elect to do drop cookies using a teaspoon. If dehydrating, flatten well to shorten time for drying.

Note: Growing up if our Nanny wanted what she called a shine to her cookies so she brushed the cookies before baking with: an egg wash (one egg whisked with a fork and brushed on with a pastry brush).

Bake on a lightly greased cookie sheet or on parchment paper laid on the cookie sheet for 20 to 25 minutes or golden brown

If you do NOT have cookie cutters, you can measure out in teaspoon size and roll into balls. Then flatten with a fork scoring the tops.

These cookies get very hard, the way dogs like them when dehydrating! HINT: Bake your cookies first and then dehydrate them for a crispier cookie without burning.

Storing: This dog cookie recipe will last in a sealed air tight container at room temperature for one week. Please practice safety first and store the cookies to stay fresh. You can even store them in the freezer for up to 4 months.

Hint & Technique

Sticky Dough: The dough for these dog treats can be sticky to work with due to the fruit and maple syrup. If your dough is too sticky just knead the dough until it becomes less sticky and add more flour to the dough continuing to knead.

ENJOY…You and YOUR DOG will love these cookies! My husband even says they are really good!

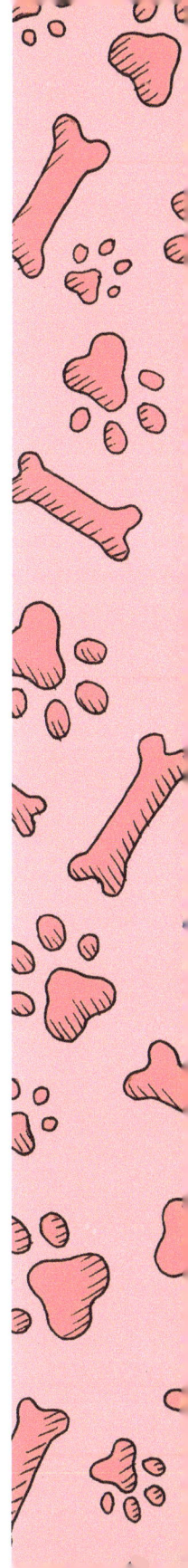

Paw Lickin' Munchies

Ingredients:

- 1 cup oat flour
- 1 ½ cups buckwheat or brown rice flour
- 2 tablespoons black strap molasses
- 2 tablespoons organic agave
- 3 eggs
- ¼ cup olive oil
- 1 teaspoon cinnamon

Directions:

Preheat oven to 350°F. Line cookie sheets with parchment paper.

Using a food processor or mixer, add flours and mix well. Add in molasses and agave. In small bowl, lightly beat egg and add the oil.

Add this mixture slowly to the food processor until a dough forms keeping sides scraped down so it remains well blended.

The dough will be soft, but be careful it is not wet. If so, add a bit of flour but it needs to remain pliable. You can either scoop it with a teaspoon for individual cookies that you may want to design or roll the dough out 1/4" thick for using your special cookie cutters We found a German Shepherd cookie cutter so you may enjoy your breed cutters as well.

Lay the cookies on oil treated cookie sheets. (parchment paper or baking mats on cookie sheets can be used instead of oil). Silicon mats are wonderful!

Bake for 30 to 35 minutes, depending your oven. Our Maggie loves her cookies crispy so we use our convection oven at the same temperature of 325°F but five to ten minutes less bake time.

Please store treats in an airtight container in the refrigerator but if you can't use in three weeks, please freeze. Safety always first.

Sweet Tater N' Salmon

Ingredients:

- 2 cans pink Salmon (need 2 cups-check weight of canned fish)
- 2 cups organic sweet potato diced, boiled, (drained, reserving 2 ½ tablespoon of liquid)
- 1 ½ cups almond flour, for a nutty flavor (oat flour works as well)
- ⅛ cup chopped fresh parsley (Remove stems before chopping)
- ⅛ cup finely chopped mint (both parsley and mint aid in digestion)
- 1 egg whip-with the reserved sweet potato liquid or 1 tablespoon water
- ½ teaspoon baking powder

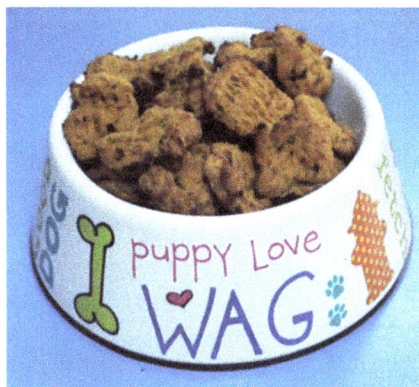

Directions:

Preheat oven to 350⁰ F.

Drain canned salmon and put in large bowl.

Break up the fish, checking for any bones.

Stir together salmon & sweet potato.

Add whipped egg, parsley, mint and baking powder, blending well.

Add sifted flour, gradually mixing.

With a spoon, use one teaspoon and drop the batter onto a greased cookie sheet. You can also use a melon baller and flatten with your fingers.

HINT: If you want to use a cookie cutter, add additional flour so the consistency is firmer for rolling out (this one we prefer to just do drop cookies so the fish is handled quicker , baked and safely stored).

Bake for 25-30 minutes until they are golden on the bottom but not dark.

OPTION: Maggie loves a cookie with a crunch as a change from soft cookies so we allow the cookies to cool and then place them in the dehydrator to dry out for a crispier cookie.

Remember this is made with fish so they must be stored in the refrigerator and used in 3 days. Freeze what you feel cannot be used in that time and always check on them before serving to your dog.

SAFETY FIRST: NEVER serve your dog what you have baked if you would not eat it yourself.

Swimmin' Salmon Dog Treats

Ingredients:

- 2 cans (14.75 oz) salmon-you can use fresh salmon. Use all the juice.
- 2 cups of rice flour-white or brown.
- 1 cup of oats
- ½ teaspoon baking powder
- ½ teaspoon dried rosemary
- ½ teaspoon oregano
- ½ teaspoon Italian seasoning
- 3 eggs
- 1 tablespoon olive oil

Directions

Preheat oven to 375°F.

Add the fish with the rest of ingredients.

Mix until well blended and shape into patties

Bake for 40 to 50 minutes or until golden brown on a parchment paper lined cookie sheet.

Let cool completely on a wire rack before serving.

Here is one you can bake for yourself and serve with rice or on a bun. For your canine family member, serve with plain white rice. Yield-eight 4.5 to5" patties.

Hint: Either buy the canned salmon without skin and bones or be prepared to remove the non meat product. Brands vary.

Banana Sweet Potato Surprise

These are a drop cookie but can be made small for training purposes.

Ingredients:

- 1 banana
- ½ cup of baked sweet potato
- ¾ cup of oat flour
- Salt-small pinch (less than 1/8 Tsp)
- ¼ tsp Ceylon cinnamon
- 1 tbsp of peanut butter with peanuts
- ½ cup of Quaker oats

Directions:

Preheat oven to 350^{0}F.

Pam cookie sheet.

Smash the banana

Bake a small sweet potato, peel and measure out 1/2 cup. Mix together banana and sweet potato. Add the rest of the ingredients.

Using a teaspoon, drop small balls onto the greased cookie sheet and make an imprint with a fork. Makes it easy to break in half for small bite sizes to use for training or on walks.

Bake for 30 to 35 minutes or until lightly browned or a bit longer for crispier cookies.

This recipe should yield 25 to 30 cookies, depending on the size you make them.

Tried and approved by Maggie :))

A HEALTHY TREAT.

Sandy Eats Remotes and Trains Her Parents
by
Rosemary "Mamie" Adkins

Our lives began (after losing our poodles) once again, the day we met Sandy. Life had been alone with emptiness all around without the love of a furry family member but we had finally decided to take that chance one more. A sweet six week old chocolate Labrador that was to be only 45 pounds full grown was who we decided to make a part of our family. We felt going from a poodle to her would not be too bad but she just kept growing! While she had her growing spurts, she certainly found a way of taking over our lives, bed and anything else she set her mind too.

Our poodles always slept with us but they were on the small size and when we adopted Sandy, we thought we would train her differently since she was to be much larger than they had been.

Meet Sandy

In the course of bringing Sandy home, we stopped to buy all the toys, food, blankets and other items the breeder had suggested for this type dog and the thought crossed our minds we also needed to purchase a playpen for her if we planned to train her not to sleep with us. A crate never even occurred to us as we had not been exposed to using one before. Excited about having her in our lives we set out to train this one correctly so we bought a playpen and set it up next to our bed, in hopes being in the room next to us, she would be happy. That is not how this went!

Sandy wanted to sleep with us, so during the night she managed to gnaw her way through the mesh on the playpen and got out finding a way up onto our beds, waking us to slobber in the faces. That night we patched the mesh, hugged her good night and hoped for the best only to awaken again being French kissed by our sweet little dog.

We knew we were in for quite a challenge so back to the pet store where we now bought an outdoor fence thinking we could gate ourselves into the waterbed. Our chests were puffed out thinking we had out foxed our newest little family member!

Have I mentioned this was the most intelligent dog we had ever had in our lives? Well, she was. Somehow, while we were slumbering in our restful states, Sandy had figured out how to open the latch we used to lock ourselves onto the bed, only this time she was quiet and simply laid between us being careful not to move a muscle so we would not notice her being on the bed. Each night this went on until we finally decided to return the fence to the pet store, defeated with no idea what to do but to give in!

Sandy had won but more than we expected. There were many nights when we slept that she must have laid there wondering what she could think up next! This was a Craftmatic bed where we used a remote for turning on and controlling extra warmth, massage and to raise and lower our head or feet. Well, you guessed it! She had the perfect plan! As she had grown a little bit older and smarter she was destined not to stay in a playpen, so she earned her stripes chewing up the remotes for our adjustable beds. Naturally the remotes had to be ordered from a distance away and we always had our beds stuck in a position not fit to sleep in, for days at a time.

We loved this wonderful soul but we were exhausted trying to outwit this innocent looking puppy!

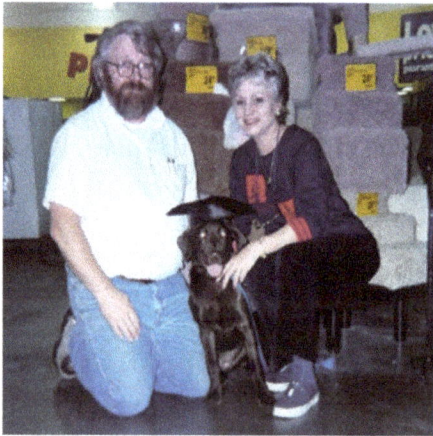

Using our remotes, every night I would raise the head and feet and at times quite high but by morning, I would lower it for just the perfect height. One morning we woke to set our beds in the down position only to discover Sandy had eaten our remote! Our bed was stuck in place with both the head and feet way up as though in a sitting position but the legs as well. It must have been fun for her as she watched the beds change position that night. But we were not laughing and we were upset when we had to crawl out of this raised bed in order to try to fix it, which of course, was impossible. At the time, the replacement was

$25 per remote but we had no choice but to get a new one, which took five days to replace with no hope of sleeping in the position we were left in thanks to our puppy!

Training was the next plan in hopes we could get her to learn chewing up our remotes was not the way of good behavior. She did graduate from this class and learning not to eat remotes did not come until we had gone through four or more replacements!

Sandy grew up becoming a gentle being, loving in every way and never was a problem from that day forward. We miss her even today because the warmth of a living soul cannot be compared to anything else. The loyalty, compassion and unconditional love was our Sandy!

Baby Nana Cookie

Make an organic and gluten free cookie for your Doggies!

Ingredients:

- 1½ cups rice flour-If you cannot find brown flour, use white or order from your market
- 6 ounce jar of organic baby food for older baby (we used banana, peach, mango but select any flavor good for your dog.
- 1 medium ripe banana-mashed
- ½ teaspoon cinnamon
- 1 tablespoon brer rabbit molasses-mild flavor

If your dough is too dry, add by teaspoon water, low sodium broth, or additional baby food for the older toddler. Infant baby food will leave the cookie tasteless

DIRECTIONS:

Pre heat your oven to 350°F.

Use a cookie sheet with Parchment paper or spray with olive oil (Canola oil or butter also works)

Using the brown rice flour, mix it with the organic baby food-if brown rice is not available, use white rice flour.

Roll into log the appropriate size for your dog. We make it 2" x 1" but reserved half of the dough mixture for cookie shape cutouts.

Cut into quarter or half inch round slices to flattened and score.

Bake on a greased cookie sheet for 10-12 minutes.

Store in the freezer after cooling holding out only what will be enjoyed in three days. Please use a good grade freezer paper so they won't freezer burn.

Additional Hint:

To create a snappier cookie we dehydrate them but we still freeze for the sake of safety what she cannot use in one week.
Their eyes will be excited and thrilled to taste the cookie you have just created just for them!

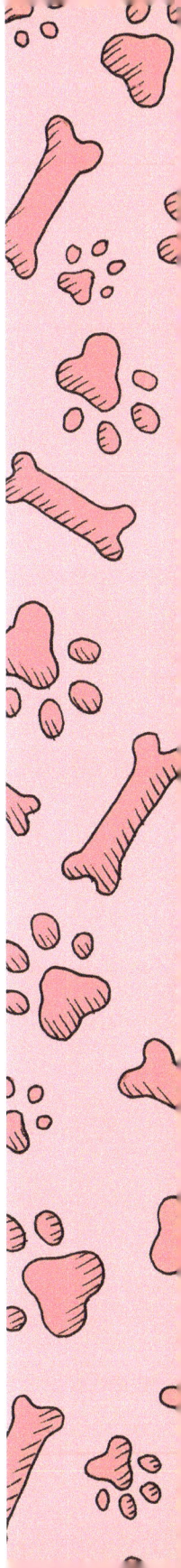

MAIN ENTREES

Maggie's Recipes come to you fresh from the oven! Your furry friends will wait by the oven eagerly for their dinner filled with only the finest human grade ingredients!

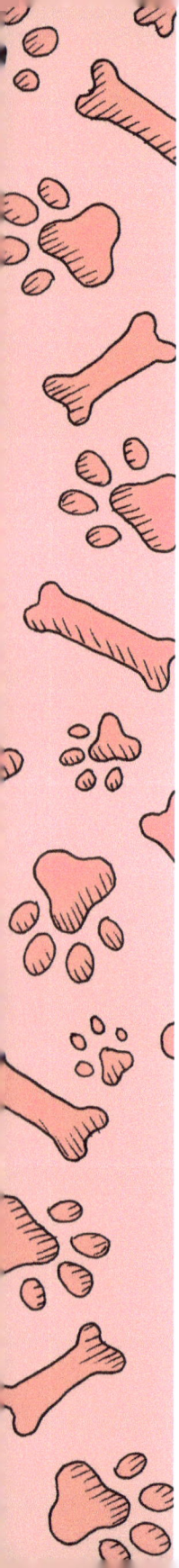

Walkin' The Dog!

by
Rosemary "Mamie" Adkins

Oh My Gosh. Have you ever walked a puppy? Which choice of the above would you like? The fresh breakfast on the right or the one the side of the road with worms crawling around it, pictured on the left? Do you remember competing with roadway trash for their attention? Then you would know all about their endless energy and their desire to walk forever, sniffing at every interesting morsel, only to get half way home and then run out of steam.

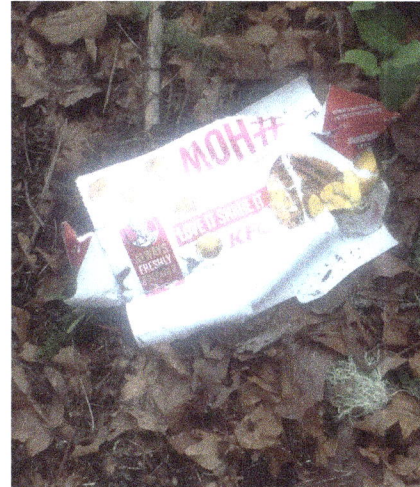

Roadside Trash

Thanks to those who litter we must deal with the curiosity of puppies learning to take a walk.

Well, Maggie would love to tell you that it is not nice to litter, because it is difficult to leave things alone when you are a puppy. Mommie and Daddy have such a stressful walk, worrying about the garbage people throw on the ground—from broken glass and soda cans to candy and cigarettes. Not to mention the parents who do not pick up their doggies' poo-poo.

This one morning, thinking we could take a walk before breakfast, we were just strolling along and boy did Maggie find a treasure of nightmares for us! People have no conscience about littering and Maggie found it all, from cigarette butts to plain garbage. Every can tossed in the ditch or each banana peel dropped on the ground became her items of interest.

"No Maggie," we would shout out. Or "Leave it!" or "Drop it!" became the only words she would hear until we could get back home. I had only taken a small amount of treats with us and it appeared she was hungry. This was unusual for her as she really was and is not a "morning person," sort of speak. But temptation was too great. As they say: *One man's trash is another's treasure* and she was out to prove that saying had merit.

Just as we could see our driveway in the not so far distance, Maggie found someone's tossed out bacon, egg and cheese muffin on the side of the road. Now, thankfully, bread does not appeal to her but the rest, well let's just say she was hungry! It was clear we needed to get home quickly before we had aged ten years from this big twenty minute walk.

Our experiences walking inspired a breakfast recipe, one that Maggie would be offered for breakfast in the morning before going for a walk and that was soon to become our routine. We also never left the house again without her favorite treat to entice her to drop whatever she decided to pick up off the road. She was not the first dog we learned this lesson from, but hey, forgetfulness is bliss when you start out on this journey anew!

I am not a morning dog - I don't want to get up.
Please hit the snooze alarm!!!

DADDY'S SCRAMBLED EGG COMBO

Ingredients:
- 2 eggs
- ¼ cup lentils
- 2 sausage links diced-mild
- 1 wedge of Laughing Cow low fat cheese

Directions:

Scramble (2) two eggs until well done

Add 1/4 cup cooked Lentils

Top with: 1/4 cup of parsley finely chopped

Dice in small pieces and lay on top of cooked eggs and lentils

1/4 wedge slice low fat Laughing Cow cheese, diced and sprinkled with low fat shredded cheddar cheese.

Cover with lid and allow heat to melt the cheese.

Cool and serve.

WOOFIN GOOD EGG SANDWICHES

Ingredients:

- 2 eggs
- 2 tablespoons milk
- 1 tablespoon chopped spinach
- 1 tablespoon diced bell pepper
- 1 tablespoon shredded carrots
- 1 tablespoon grated low fat Romano cheese
- 1 tablespoon grated low fat Swiss cheese

NOTE: You can use any cheese you like and 2 tablespoons of one kind if you like-just be sure you use low fat cheese for your dogs well being.

Directions:

Mix eggs and milk together and blend well

Add remaining ingredients mixing well until they are fluffy and light. I like to use an electric mixer so the egg mixture is fluffy.

TO BAKE:

Using a sandwich maker, spray with olive oil cooking spray and heat until ready for mixture. Add batter to the sandwich maker and close the iron cooking until done.

Eggs will form like a sandwich and be oh so good. Cheeses may vary but again, always use low fat to watch for those extra calories your dog does not need. We cook them until the sandwich is a bit crunchy since our dog loves everything that crunches.

Chicky Chicken Loaf

Ingredients:

- 3 ½ pounds boneless skinless chicken breast
- 1 medium zucchini
- 1 medium yellow crookneck squash
- 1 small bell pepper-any color
- 1 small bunch fresh spinach
- ½ lb. fresh green beans
- 1 large carrot
- 1 small sweet potato
- 7 cups dry oats
- 2 eggs
- 1 can of low sodium chicken broth
- 2 tablespoons of olive oil-may also use canola oil
- ⅛ teaspoon garlic
- ½ tablespoon Italian seasoning
- Cooking spray
- Jumbo muffin pan or desired size for servings

Directions:

Hint: Gather all ingredients so you are sure to have what you need before you begin.

Preheat oven to 350^{0}F and using cooking spray, grease the inside of a jumbo muffin pan.

Chop all vegetables in tiny diced pieces.

Bring a pot of water to a boil and then add all vegetables.

Cook for 4 minutes-take off burner.

While vegetables are steaming in a covered pan off the stove, use a meat grinder and process the chicken breast on fine grind.

Once chicken is ready set aside leaving it in the mixer

Drain water from vegetables and using a potato masher-mash the vegetables until chunky but also with a smooth texture.

Add the chicken, vegetables and all seasonings including the eggs and two tablespoons oil.

After blending well, add oats a small amount at a time so it is mixed well.

Make chicken balls in approximately 6 ounce portions and placing them into the muffin pan and gently pat them down to fill the muffin cavities leaving a small area around and on top of them.

Add one tablespoon of low sodium chicken broth to each cavity.

Bake for 45 minutes or until internal temperature is 180°F. Please be aware ovens and areas vary in cooking time so be watchful they don't overcook or burn.

* Use of garlic is a controversy amongst most veterinarians and animal care personnel but we spoke with our Veterinarian and his opinion was the use of this garlic was not harmful nor the quantity. Use your own judgment as this recipe can easily leave it out. It is said to have many benefits.

EYES GLAZED OVER BEEFY BEEF HEART

Ingredients:

- 3 pounds beef heart
- ¼ cup olive oil
- 1 tablespoon Italian seasoning
- pinch of sea salt
- pinch of Garlic Lovers Garlic

Directions:

Remove all excess fat.

Slice meat paper thin.

Hint

For easier slicing-freeze the beef heart until slightly frozen.

If your knives are not exceptionally sharp this can be a difficult task and you may want to ask your butcher to cut it for you.

As you slice the heart, place the pieces in a large bowl so you have ample room to marinate.

After the heart is completely sliced, add the oil and seasoning to the bowl and toss well.

Cover with plastic wrap and refrigerate for two hours.

Remove from the refrigerator and lay on the dehydrator rack with the insert (if available with your dehydrator) in single layers so NOT to touch.

Set your dehydrator according to manufacturer's recommendation for beef.

Maggie's eyes are fixed and glazed over with excitement when she even hears the name "EYES GLAZED OVER BEEF HEART".

This is one recipe I don't share with her but she tells us we can have some too!

This is what we call a high value treat. Sometimes Maggie focuses on something that she shouldn't have and won't give it up. High value treats to the rescue.

Jet Goes Garden Grazing

by

Martha Char Love

When I was seven years old, I got my first dog and named him Jet. I earned him by crawling under my neighbor's house (a very small crawl space that none of the adults could go through) and getting out a litter of newly born puppies before the neighbor called the Humane Society to come capture what he considered "wild puppies" and take them away. In the 50s, puppies being taken away in such a circumstance would have not had a happy ending. But if the puppies were brought out from under the house early in their lives, the neighbor said they would be okay for pets. Not wanting any harm to come to the puppies, I crawled my way past the dark corners and scary spider webs and pulled out each puppy, one by one. And for the task of rescuing them, I was rewarded the opportunity of first pick of whichever puppy I wanted and I am sure to this day that I selected the best dog ever!

I named my rescued puppy Jet (I liked jet airplanes and he had a beautiful jet black coat) and as he got older and wiser, I taught him to sit upon command using store bought treats. If you were a dog owner during the 50s, you may remember the little round store-bought dog treats that came in a box and were different colors. I loved giving them to Jet and for a long time, I thought the green ones must taste like lime, the red ones like strawberries, etc. But one day, I tasted a few of them and to my disappointment, they all tasted the same. But Jet loved them and didn't care that they were the same. So if you find a particular dog treat in our book that you like making and your dog likes eating, don't worry about making it over and over again. Many dogs don't seem to mind eating something they like day after day.

Also, Jet liked eating red tomatoes straight out of my father's tomato patch (sorry, Dad!). Sometimes he would eat the strawberries too. He loved garden grazing! I would only let him eat one of each garden delight a day and then I'd call him away so my father didn't start missing tomatoes and strawberries. I would think that one of the healthiest dog treats would be those grazed fresh from your organic garden, plot or pot. Although many people go to great lengths to train their dogs to stay out of gardens, you might try growing tomatoes and strawberries just to explore if your dog would like these garden delights as treats. If you don't want your dog in your garden, you can always grow the food that is just for your dog in pots and teach him/her to eat only out of them and leave the rest of the garden alone. Be sure your dog eats the ripe fruits and vegetables and stays away from eating the stems, seeds and leaves that are poisonous!

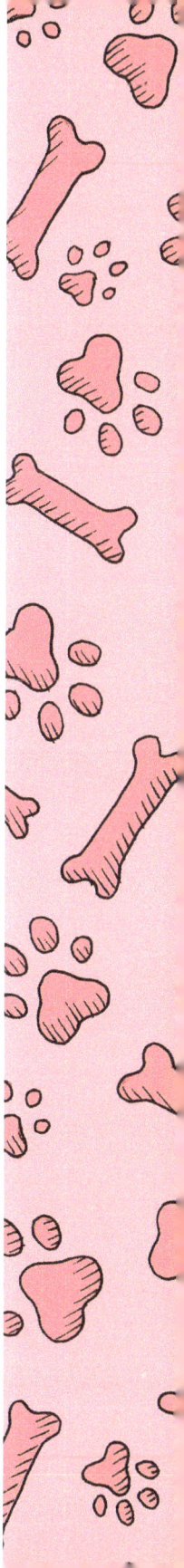

Buddy Bean and Beef Burgers

This recipe is inspired by the memory of my dog Jet who loved tomatoes. If you need to leave out the egg in the recipe, you may do so. I have made this recipe both ways and it works fine with or without the egg. I added it mostly for extra nutrition, as eggs are good for most dogs' coats if they are not allergic to them. Also, this recipe would not be advised for the rare dog that is allergic to nightshade plants like tomatoes.

Ingredients:

- 1 cup ground beef (about 1/3 lb. of lean beef)
- ¼ cup gabanzo bean flour
- 1 teaspoon dried parsley
- 1 medium egg
- 1 tablespoon water
- 2 tablespoons tomato paste (with no salt added) or substitute one small diced fresh tomato and leave out the water.

Directions:

Preheat oven to 350° F.

Cook, drain ground beef, lightly pat with paper towel and set aside.

Mix together the flour and parsley.

Add to this mixture the cooked beef.

Beat the egg separately and add to it the water and tomato. Mix well.

Pour the egg and tomato mixture into the beef mixture and stir until completely combined.

On a lightly oiled (we use olive oil) baking sheet, spoon out mixture with large spoon (about ¼ cup) and then flatten into cake patties. If you are preparing these for a small dog, use a little less mixture.

Bake for about 15 minutes or until done and cool.

MR. GREENIE EARNS COOKIES

by
Rosemary "Mamie" Adkins
and
Douglas Adkins

Since we first adopted Maggie, we have enjoyed delightful conversations with all the usual joy and charm as can be expected between a Mommy and her baby. Even though Maggie's vocabulary is limited to three words…woof, woof, woof…we do share a perfect understanding and there is little doubt that she knows every word we are saying to her.

Remembering Maggie's intense illness and fear as an abused puppy we are now so happy to watch her play in ways she never would have done in those first few months. So now that the communications are wide open with her the games she plays just light up our hearts with joy she seems to no longer live in such fear.

One of Maggie's favorite things to play is our "Mr. Greenie" (ball game) and here is how it usually goes:

"What's the matter with my baby? Come on, Maggie and tell Mommy!"

Maggie sits there silently waiting for my next move. I then go about my business at the kitchen center island when suddenly; I feel a gentle shove at the back of my knees. I turn to see what's happening and there's Maggie with her Mr. Greenie in her mouth and making an attempt to utter her usual 'woof'! That muted 'woof' seems to demand my attention and of course, it must be right now! In the spirit of fun, I keep the game going and tell her, "I can't understand you, Maggie! Let's just go and sit down and you can sit on my lap and tell me what's on your mind!"

So up she jumps onto my lap and proceeds to stare intently down onto the ball. Maggie shifts her attention back and forth between me and the ball as if to say, "C'mon Mommy, let's keep playing this game!" Well, we all know how persistent some men in our lives can be (*and I suppose women too*), so I say to Maggie, "Okay, let's name our ball Mr. Greenie or Mr. Green Ball!" Immediately Maggie sits straight up as if to indicate her approval. Then she jumps down from my lap and grabs Mr. Greenie in her mouth and tears around the house from room to room, as she grips her toy tightly but ever so tenderly in her mouth.

Later, as I prepare dinner, that ever so familiar 'woof, woof, woof' greets me again. "Now what, Maggie? Oh, you want to play with Mr. Greenie again? OK, but let's have dinner first." This is a pivotal point in our game. Right on cue, Maggie drops Mr. Greenie on the floor at my feet and joins me to be hand fed her dinner that I have lovingly cooked especially for her which we have done for months in order to nurse her back to health. She's not spoiled so no thoughts like that one—ok? She's just intensely loved.

Tonight Maggie dines on her favorite chicken breast dinner laced with tomatoes and Italian spices and made so her parents can have it as well. She knows dinner is important and playing Mr. Greenie won't happen until she eats.

But little Miss Maggie has her parents trained very well. Once dinner is over for her parents, she begins to *Woof* again. Mommie looks at Maggie and says, "Maggie, you have not finished your dinner and you need to eat for your strength. Well, ok, Daddy will take it to the front room and you can play Mr. Greenie and each time you bring him back, you must eat another bite." Maggie is so happy she runs to get Mr. Greenie and sits by her Daddy for her first bite. "What a good little girl," Daddy says to her. "Now go get Greenie and bring him back."

Maggie now knows there is always a reward for finishing her dinner and we never dare forget it either. Our after dinner games begin! Now Mommie and Daddy are on the floor where Daddy throws the ball and Maggie fetches it and takes it to Mommie for her cookie, hugs, and lots of kisses. Then the cycle continues with Mommie tossing the ball to

Daddy and he throws it off into the distance for her to fetch and bring back to Mommie. All in all a family night of fun!

Well, you should see her peel rubber when we toss her ball into the living room!

Italiano Chick Chick

Ingredients:

- 6 skinless, boneless chicken breast
- 15 ounce can of peach slices in lite syrup
- 2 - 12 ounce cans of stewed tomatoes (no onions)
- 3 tablespoons olive oil
- pinch of salt
- 1 tablespoon Italian seasoning
- ¼ teaspoon garlic seasoning

Directions:

In a skillet brown the chicken breast in olive oil until browned.

Add peaches with juice and simmer until liquid is gone. Either remove and discard peaches or cook with chicken for a bit more peach flavor.

Now add the stewed tomatoes. (chop the tomatoes in small size pieces)

Cook for ten minutes and remove.

Oven:

Put in baking pan and cover baking at 350°F for 30 minutes.

Remove foil cover and bake another 20 minutes.

Unless you have hungry doggies, this recipe is enough to share with a family of four.

Serve over rice or noodles for the humans in your home but for your doggie, they can have brown rice with their chicken dinner. Alternative suggestion, try serving with potato and green beans.

Buff N' Stuff Stew

Ingredients:

- 1 pound of lean stew meat
- 1 cup rice flour
- 1 large sweet potato-sliced like steak fries
- 1 small bag of baby carrots
- 1 small bell pepper (it does matter which color)
- ½ pound green beans
- 1 small white potato
- 4 cups low sodium beef broth-add additional water as required for consistency.
- 1 bunch of asparagus for a side dish
- ½ cup olive oil
- Pinch of salt
- ⅛ teaspoon garlic lovers garlic
- 1 tablespoon Italian seasoning

Directions:

Rinse meat with cool water and place on cutting board. Pat dry with paper towels.

Trim off excess fat. Cut into bit size pieces. (stew meat never seems to come in small bite sizes)

Coat meat on all sides with flour and add to the skillet so the pieces don't touch and brown on all sides. Don't be afraid of using lots of flour, this will produce a nice gravy.

Add seasonings, reserving ½ teaspoon of Italian Seasoning to sprinkle on noodles if desired.

If needed, more oil can be added.

In an electric skillet or stove top skillet, heat the oil on high and turn it back to 350^{0}F once skillet is hot.

Wash vegetables, cut into bite size pieces before adding to skillet, adding all vegetables at one time.

NOTE:

Now is when you decide if you want to use a slow cooker or large skillet.

If using a slow cooker, cook on medium for 4 to 5 hours depending on your altitude and cooker.

Stove top skillet will require closer attention so as not to burn and needs to cook at 350^0F for a few hours.

Add your vegetables, and cook the required amount of time.

Add water to cover and any extra flour to thicken your gravy.

This recipe can be enjoyed by the entire family so we will sometimes add a side of fresh asparagus for ourselves and furry friends.

Serve with Noodles or rice if desired.

Maggie, Sleeping Angel

by

Rosemary "Mamie" Adkins

Is it possible that a 10 week-old puppy can save a life?

Tic toc, tic toc. Time seemed to be running out for me, but Maggie, determined to save my life, resorted to becoming ill herself.

Maggie Anne had awakened as my blood sugar (I am a diabetic) dropped to a dangerous low, and then she began to whine in a strange way. I could hear her but was too ill to respond. Maggie had whimpered until she became frustrated in her desperation to wake me. It was a life threatening situation, but she was a puppy of only 10 weeks of age. Not knowing what else to do Maggie began to violently vomit in her crate until I awoke enough to help her. Our instincts were so strong to help one another, that within moments of her retching, both Doug and I were awake enough to get me the help I needed. Maggie, of course, stopped retching the moment we arose.

After sharing this story with two trainers it was determined that though Maggie was only a puppy, she needed a job to keep her precious and active mind from getting bored. Hence, she was headed for school. Little Miss Maggie Anne worked so hard trying to be that perfect student (while really wanting to play with the other schoolmates). By the time school was out it was nap time for our precious angel, followed by a dinner full of protein to help her gain back her energy to begin again!

117

Beefy Beef Loaf

Ingredients:

- 3 ½ pounds lean ground beef
- 1 medium zucchini
- 1 medium yellow crookneck squash
- 1 small bell pepper-any color
- 1 small bunch fresh spinach
- 1/2 lb. fresh green beans
- 1 large carrot
- 1 small sweet potato
- 7 cups dry oats
- 2 eggs
- 1 can of low sodium beef broth
- 2 tablespoons of olive oil
- ⅛ teaspoon garlic
- ½ tablespoon Italian seasoning
- cooking spray
- Jumbo muffin pan or desired size for servings

(all vegetables are organic)

Directions:

Hint: Gather all ingredients so you are sure to have what you need before you begin.

Preheat oven to 350°F and using a cooking spray grease the inside of a jumbo muffin pan.

Chop all vegetables in tiny diced pieces.

Bring a pot of water to a boil and then add all vegetables.

Cook for 4 minutes—take off burner.

While vegetables are steaming in a covered pan off the stove, use a meat grinder and process the beef on fine grind.

Once beef is ready set aside leaving it in the mixer.

Drain water from vegetables and using a potato masher mash the vegetables until chunky but also with a smooth texture.

Add the beef, vegetables and all seasonings including the eggs and two tablespoons oil.

After blending well, add oats a small amount at a time so it is mixed well

Make beef balls in approximately 6 ounce portions, placing them into the muffin pan and gently patting them down to fill the muffin cavities, leaving a small area around and on top of them

Add one tablespoon of low sodium beef broth to each cavity

Bake for 45 minutes or until internal temperature is 160-170 degrees. Please be aware ovens and areas vary in cooking time so be watchful they don't overcook or burn.

* Use of garlic is a controversy amongst most veterinarians and animal care personnel but we spoke with our Veterinarian and his opinion was the use of this garlic was not harmful nor the quantity. Use your own judgment as this recipe can easily leave it out. It is said to have many beneficial benefits.

Pancake Puffs

So good, you will want one for yourself!

Ingredients:

- 2 eggs
- 1 tablespoon milk
- 1 apple-cored, peeled, diced small
- pinch to ⅓ teaspoon cinnamon

Directions:

Crack eggs in a mixing bowl.

Add milk and whip until fluffy.

Blend apple pieces with cinnamon and blend well.

In a sandwich maker, ladle in egg mixture on both sides of cooker leaving the cooker open and flat.

Once the mixture is set, add the apples and cinnamon on one side and close to finish cooking. Watch closely so it does not burn.

Option:

Add 1 teaspoon of low fat cream cheese, as in Laughing Cow cheese, when you add the apple mixture.

WARNING:

The apples will be very hot so let completely cool before feeding to your dog.

EaRth ShakiN' Paw LickiN' chow

Ingredients:

- 2 pounds ground turkey breast. (Can use chicken for substitute)
- 1 large organic sweet potato (see cooking instructions below)
- 1 large egg.
- 4 cups rolled oats.

Directions:

Preheat oven to 400° F.

Mix the **ground turkey meat with the** rest of the ingredients. This mixture should be thick and but not wet, like a meat loaf.

Place in a greased glass baking pan. Should fit into a 10" square pan.

Bake covered for 40 minutes and then uncovered for another 10 minutes, allowing it to brown. Timing depends on your oven and altitude, but be careful not to overcook.

Cool completely, slice and serve.

* Sweet Potatoes: peel, cube and boil until done. Drain and mash adding ¼ teaspoon of cinnamon (Ceylon) and 1 teaspoon butter. The cinnamon with butter adds a flavor to the turkey that entices your doggie to enjoy their new meal!

Now you are set for the week!

Eggstravagent Meal

Ingredients:

- 2 eggs
- 1 tablespoon milk
- 1 teaspoon chopped spinach
- 1 teaspoon diced bell pepper
- 1 teaspoon shredded carrots
- 1 teaspoon grated low fat Romano cheese
- 1 teaspoon grated low fat Swiss cheese

Directions:

Mix eggs and milk together and whip well.

Add remaining ingredients until well blended continuing to whip so fluffy and light.

Using a sandwich maker, spray with olive oil cooking spray and heat until ready for mixture. Close the iron, cooking until done.

Eggs will form like a sandwich and will be oh so good. Cheeses may vary but always use low fat to watch for those extra calories your dog does not need.

SPECIAL DAYS

THE GANG'S ALL HERE! COME CELEBRATE YOUR BIRTHDAYS, HOLIDAYS OR WHATEVER DAY WITH A NEW RECIPE. ANY OCCASION IS GOOD FOR A SPECIAL DAY. BE SURE TO ADD AN APPETIZER TO THESE DAYS TOO! JUST HAVING A FURRY FRIEND MEANS A SPECIAL DAY IN EVERYONE'S LIFE!

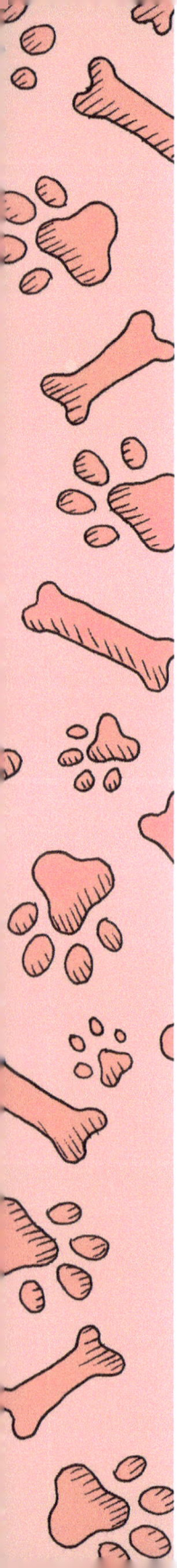

ALOHA

by

Martha Char Love

Aloha (to the right) decked out in her bridal Halloween costume is awaiting by Auntie Martha's stove for her fresh baked carrots and chicken biscuits:

Aloha's Trick

I like to experiment with varying the cooking time on cookie treats, affecting how soft and crunchy they are to eat. And then I like to see which type my dogs enjoy the most. So far, both Aloha and Momo love them all, but Aloha finds the softer cookies easier to chew for her little mouth.

The other day, Aloha's mom, our neighbor Diane, asked her if she wanted to go see "auntie and uncle." This is a trick that Diane has used every day for about two years to get Aloha to willingly want to come upstairs where our apartments are located (as otherwise Aloha would want to stay all day in the dog park built conveniently behind our apartment building). Being a Hawaiian resident dog, an adorable black Chihuahua, she has lots of what we in Hawaii call "uncles" and "aunts," which is everyone who is friendly. But Aloha only knows one "aunt AND uncle" set, so she knows exactly who Diane is speaking of when she says "Want to go see Auntie and Uncle?" In fact, sometimes, Diane will simply say, "Do you want to go see "AND?" and Aloha will head for the gate of the park, ready to convene at our place.

125

Besides daily petting and throwing her toys for her to fetch, she knows there could be dog treats at "AND's" place. Since she is such a small dog, I have found that she likes the treats that I cook to be not too crunchy. It just makes chewing them easier for her with her little mouth. If I make them too hard for her, she will only eat the cookies if we humans act like we will eat the treat if she does not. And sometimes I wonder who is tricking who, since she ends up with all the cookies anyway!

Aloha loves carrots. She does not particularly like fish, so I came up with the following special treat with carrots and chicken that she loves to eat. If Aloha ever decides on a proper suitor (of which she has many), Diane is planning to have me cater in these Love Cookies at her Luau wedding in the dog park of our apartment building.

Aloha's Wedding Day Love Cookies

If your dog does not like fish but loves chicken and also carrots, try this special recipe of Love Cookies. They come Aloha approved.

Ingredients:

- ½ cup mashed and drained cooked carrots (I usually microwave a few baby carrots in a dish with some water)
- ½ cup chopped and cooked collards (cut in small pieces without center rib of leaf)
- 1 teaspoon olive oil or coconut oil
- ½ cup small pieces of chicken (use the can chicken so it is soft and mushy, but be sure to wash and drain any salt off that may be added in the can ingredients)
- 1 tablespoon water (use water left over from cooking carrots)
- 1 medium egg
- ½ cup almond flour (or substitute wheat or buckwheat flour)
- ½ cup oat flour (or substitute buckwheat flour to make grain-free)

Directions:

Preheat oven to 350°F.

Mix the cooked carrots, collards, oil, chicken, water and egg together.

Add the flours together in a separate bowl, stir and then add it to the carrot mixture. Knead with your hands until mixed completely and the dough softens.

The oat flour should make it easy to smash out dough on a floured surface and use a cookie cutter to make shapes. If you are making this grain free (leaving out the oat flour), just drop a tablespoon of batter on the cookie sheet and smash flat with wet hand or spoon, as they will probably not roll out as well. Your dog will not care if they are not in recognizable shapes.

Bake about 18 to 20 minutes, until dough is only slightly hardened. Remember that it will cook and harden after you have taken it out of the oven.

Let them cool before serving. Aloha!

Magic and Elfie Decide to Change Their Diets

by

Martha Char Love

Have you ever heard of dogs suddenly changing their dietary likes and dislikes? Well, both of our dogs did this and, strangely, both decided to make the change at the same time.

We were once told by a vet that popcorn makes a great treat for dogs and that it is best to sprinkle some nutritional yeast on it for additional health benefits. (We have also read in a dog magazine that popcorn contains potassium as well as the bone-building minerals phosphorous, magnesium, and calcium, and it is good for dogs.) We tried for over 10 years to give popcorn as a treat to our dogs Magic and Elfie, but neither would have anything to do with it (with or without the yeast). One day, after living in the same house for years, we had to move across town. Very soon after we arrived in our new house, we made some popcorn. We had long given up trying to feed it to Magic and Elfie, but some accidentally fell on the floor from someone's bowl and both dogs began rushing around with their noses on the ground and quickly gobbled it all up! Somehow, moving across town had changed their taste for this healthy food and they ate it readily from that day forth.

Another odd thing that happened at that same time is that Magic started pulling rubber ducks out of the bathtub and carrying them around as if they were her babies. Up until that time, she had never noticed that the ducks existed. Neither did she ever want to play with any dog toys.

Anyway, in honor of dogs like Magic and Elfie who like corn, we have included a recipe we call "Holiday Duckies," with corn as one of the ingredients. They are made with a Duckie cookie cutter Miss Maggie Ann sent me last Christmas.

128

Holiday Duckies

These treats are made with corn, peas, and green beans (fresh or frozen organics), so be sure that your dog can tolerate and likes these ingredients (some dogs are allergic to peas and corn). I made these as an Easter treat for my neighbor dogs and they all loved them. There is not much corn in them however, just enough for the taste and you can substitute other healthy vegetables for the corn if you think it best for your dog.

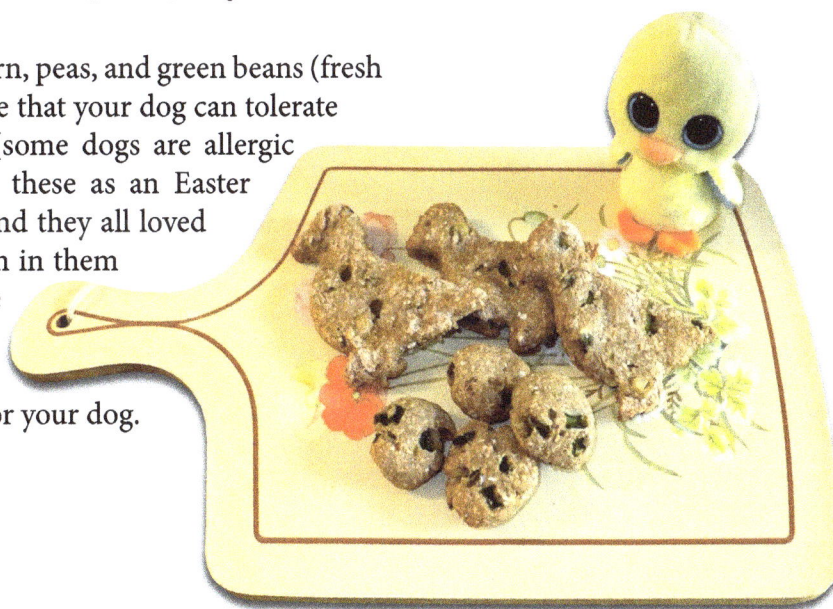

Duckies with eggs - a great
Easter and Spring holiday treat

Ingredients:

- ½ cup cooked corn, smashed
- ½ cup cooked peas, smashed
- ½ cup green beans, diced in small pieces
- 1 medium egg
- ¼ tablespoon olive oil
- ½ cup whole wheat or Quinoa (or buckwheat flour*)
- ¾ cup rolled oat flour
- 1 teaspoon crushed rosemary

*You may need 1 tablespoon of water if you use buckwheat as it is heavier flour.

Directions:

Preheat oven to 325⁰F.

Combine the corn and peas in a bowl and smash them with a fork. Add the diced green beans.

Now add the egg and oil to the vegetables.

In a separate bowl, add flours and rosemary and then add to vegetable mixture.

Knead dough (use hands) until well mixed and stays held together.

Divide the dough in half. On a floured surface, roll out the first half to ¼ inch thick. Cut out cookies using a 2 inch duckie shaped cookie cutter (wet the cutter). Place on lightly oiled cookie baking sheet.

Bake about 18 to 20 minutes.

Paw Berry Delicious

This special cookie is made from our hearts for Maggie-from her family

Ingredients:

- 2 cups oat flour
- ⅓ ancient grain gluten free flour or any organic flour
- 8 oz low fat cream cheese
- 1 cup diced strawberries
- ¼ cup water
- dash of cinnamon
- 1 tablespoon agave

Directions:

Preheat oven to 375^0 F.

Prepare cookie sheet with parchment paper or cooking spray.

In a medium bowl, blend together flours.

In a food processor, blend together cream cheese, strawberries and water until whipped, as in a pudding.

Add this mixture to the flours and blend well adding additional flour, if too sticky.

Put dough on the floured surface of a cutting board or counter top.

Knead dough and roll out to ⅛" to ¼" thickness, whichever you prefer.

Using your favorite cookie cutters, cut out cookies and place on prepared cookie sheet.

Prior to baking, sprinkle cinnamon on top of each cookie, at your option.

Bake on center rack for 15 to 18 minutes or until golden brown around the edges. Be careful not to burn these cookies.

After cookies have cooled, put them on wire cookie racks to completely cool down before serving. Store in air tight containers.

We always use organic ingredients where available and filtered water.

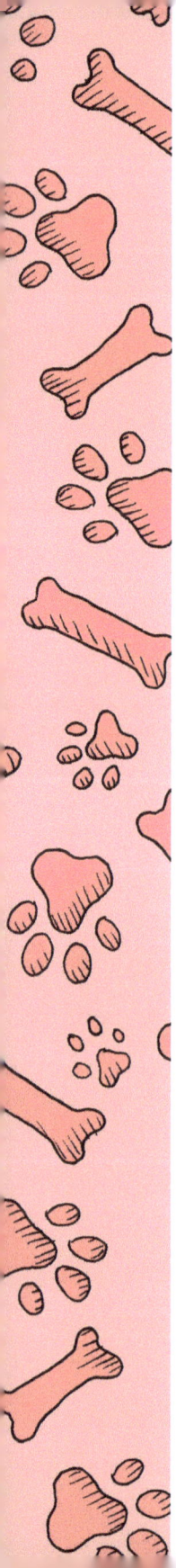

SICK DAYS

These are days to be watchful for nutrition and lots of fluids. Here we offer healthy treats, porridge or rice dishes to calm tummies. A little play or special attention with a spoonful of love never hurts anyone! Be sure to check with your veterinarians.

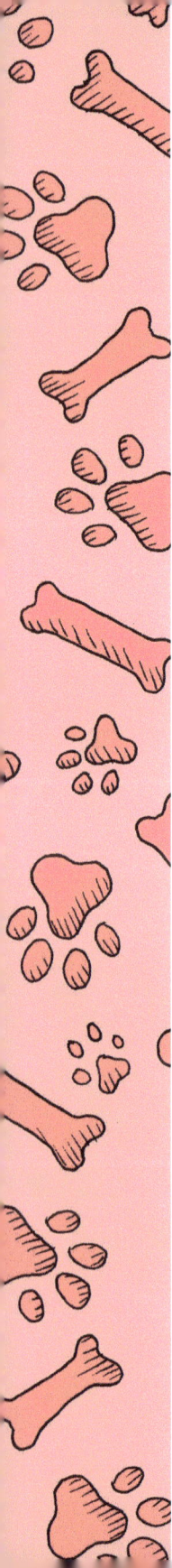

ELFIE: A KING OF A DOG WITH A SENSITIVE TUMMY

by

Martha Char Love

Elfie was a regal and brilliant white shepherd, who held his head high, pranced light on his feet and moved like a stallion on his walks. We always let him pick the direction of his nightly walks, that is, which direction on neighborhood streets to take each night. But for all his kingliness, he could really not eat like one and could only eat cheap dried dog food with a lot of filler ingredients in it—all the expensive brands were too rich for him and made him sick, even when slowly introduced into his diet.

We often remarked that Elfie was so high-spirited that he did not need much nutrition to live on and best survived off sunlight. Store bought dog treats just did not work for him either. It never occurred to us to try making his treats at home. And I do not know what would have worked best for his digestive system if I had pursued this idea. But if he were here with us today, I would certainly experiment with seeing how easily digested foods like sweet potatoes would work for him as a treat.

It is important to point out that Elfie lived until nearly 16 years old and ate cheap dried dog food for dinner up until the night before the morning he died a natural and peaceful death at home. So, take your cues from your dog's personal digestive system and don't fear to give him what works for his particular body. For one reason or another, be it a sensitive digestive track like with Elfie or food allergies like with Momo (yes, dogs can have food allergies just like people) or just personal taste choices, some of the treats in our book may not work for your particular dog. But we think we have included enough variety so that you can find a few tailored just for your good boy or girl!

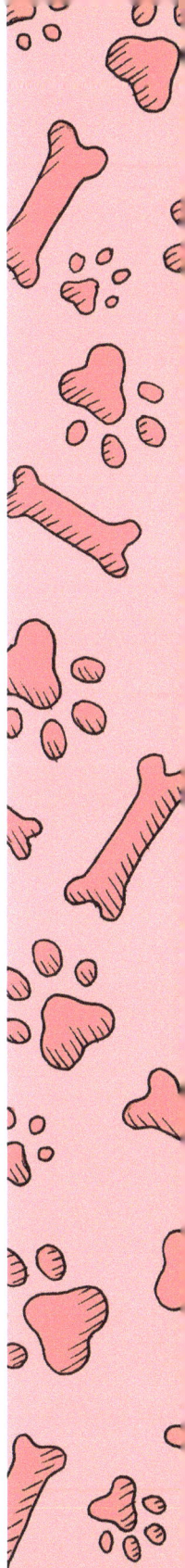

Pooches Porridge

Ingredients:

- cream of wheat
- 4 ounces cooked chicken diced small (we like to bake or grill the chicken)
- ¼ cup blueberries (If your dog is real sick, leave the fruit out)
- Pinch of cinnamon

Directions:

Follow recommended recipe for two people and prepare the cream of wheat (please do not use instant as the nutritional values are greatly lost).

Once cereal is cooked, add the cooked chicken and blueberries.

Mix well and let stand 15 minutes to cool. Be sure it is completely cool before serving.

Variations:

The same dish can be prepared using oatmeal.

¼ fresh banana diced into small pieces.

This is a great meal to try on Sick Days. You can double the batch so you are able to feed small portions several times a day, but making it in small batches keeps it fresh for each feeding.

DOUG'S CORNER

MAGGIE AND I HAD JUST COME INSIDE AFTER SHE HAD DONE HER EVENING CONSTITUTIONAL. I WAS SITTING ACROSS FROM MAMIE AND NOTICED THAT MAGGIE WAS CHEWING ON HER BONE, OR SO I THOUGHT. I THEN NOTICED THAT ONE OF MAMIE'S FEET WAS BARE AND ONE WAS NOT. MAMIE DIDN'T NOTICE BECAUSE SHE TENDS TO RUB HER FOOT AND IT JUST CAME OFF WITHOUT HER KNOWING. CHECKED OUT MAGGIE AND I COULD JUST SEE SOMETHING WHITE STICKING OUT OF HER MOUTH. IT TOOK A PIECE OF "EYES GLAZED OVER BEEF HEART" OUT OF THE FRIG TO RESCUE HER BRAND NEW SOCK BACK. IT WAS PRETTY WET SO IT WASN'T GOING BACK ON THE NOW BARE FOOT. INTO THE LAUNDRY IT WENT.

ELFIE'S Easy Tummy cookies

This snack is filled with fiber, vitamin A, beta-carotene, iron and potassium and the sweet potatoes and ginger make it a good treat for a dog like Elfie with a sensitive tummy. Oats also help with digestion in senior dogs.

Ingredients:

- 1 cup mashed cooked sweet potoates (peeled)
- 2 tablespoons unsulphured black strap molasses
- ¼ tablespoon olive oil
- 1 cup whole oats flour (or substitute ½ cup with brown rice flour)
- ¼ teaspoon baking soda
- ¼ teaspoon baking powder
- ½ teaspoon powered ginger

Directions:

Preheat oven to 350⁰F.

Mix sweet potatoes, black strap molasses, filtered water, and olive oil together in a small mixing bowl (remember that these cookies will freeze in small batches so select a medium bowl if you double the recipe).

Add the flour, baking soda, baking powder, then the ginger to the mixture and knead until mixed completely and the dough softens.

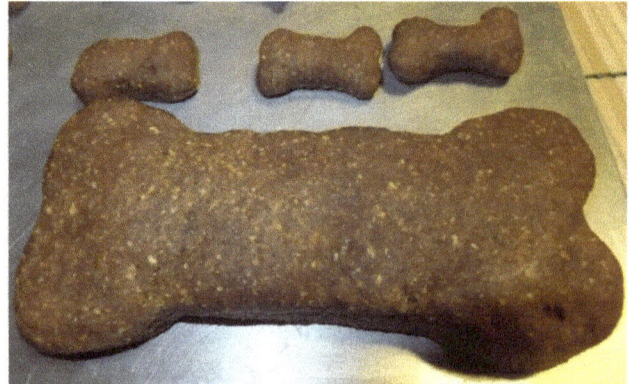

A King's Treat

Place dough on a flat floured surface for rolling out. Using your hands, flatten the dough out to ½ inch thick. Using a large cookie cutter (I like the bone cutters shown in the picture below), cut out cookies and place on a lightly oiled cookie sheet. You may need to add a little more oat flour to make it easier to roll out dough.

Bone cookie cutters

Bake about 25 minutes, until dough is slightly hardened. Remember that it will cook and harden a little when first taken out of the oven.

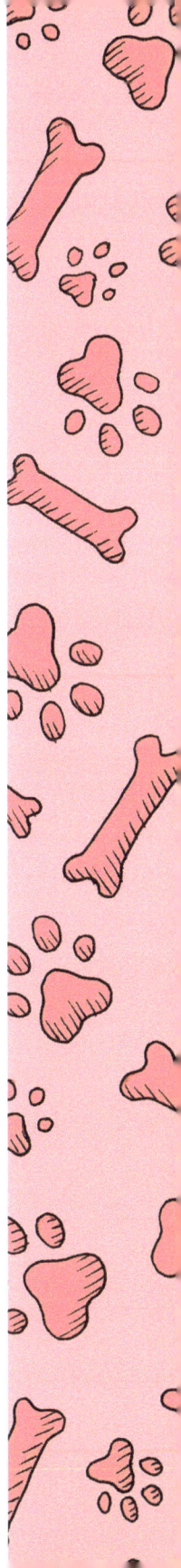

Bow Wow Sick Day Chow

These are special days when everyone is upset because your doggie isn't feeling good.

Ingredients:

- 2 pounds extra lean ground beef
- 2 cups rice
- 1 tablespoon butter
- 4 cups of filtered water
- 1 teaspoon of salt. Your dogs don't need salt but on sick days we have been told they should get a small amount in their diet, especially if vomiting, but we advise you consult your own veterinarian for guidance.
- Three cans low sodium chicken broth
- 2 ice cube trays
- Wheel barrel full of hugs

Directions:

Before cooking the ground beef start your rice.

Combine your rice, butter, water and salt cooking in whatever method you usually do. If using a rice cooker, cook until done, following the manufacturer's instructions.

Prepare your ground beef and add it to a hot skillet with a small amount of olive oil.

Cook until done in small pieces as though making taco meat.

Add the ground beef to the rice and continue cooking the rice until the timer on your rice cooker goes off.

Allow to cool to just warm and serve with your barrel of hugs!

Sick Days

On sick days it's important to take care your dog is drinking water so for added precaution, we prepare ice cubes with a low sodium broth. Be sure you cook the broth bringing it to a boil before using. Allow to cool and then add broth to the ice cube trays and freeze.

HINTS:

If you have fresh mint or parsley, consider making a few cubes with a very small amount of diced mint to settle the stomach. Parsley in small amounts can be added to the broth before freezing to also aid in their digestion.

I would suggest you lay a towel down on the floor before giving them the ice cube.

Feed in many small portions so not to overfeed a sick tummy.

Chicken breast cut up in small pieces without skin or fat is a great substitute for ground beef and is easier for them to digest. You can also use the broth (from when you boil the chicken) to make the ice cubes.

Again, please consult your own veterinarian for advice as to how best to care for your dog on a sick day.

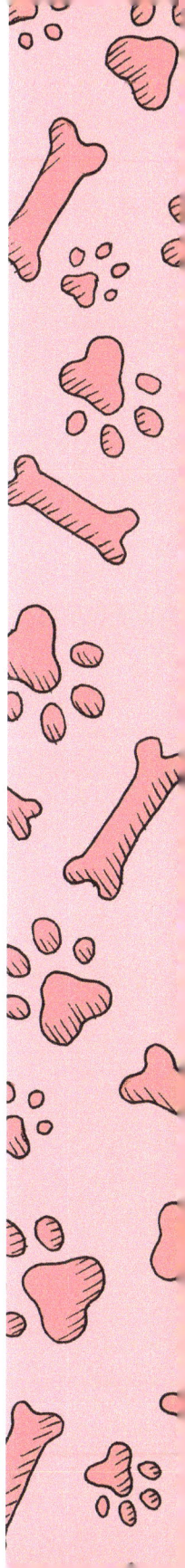

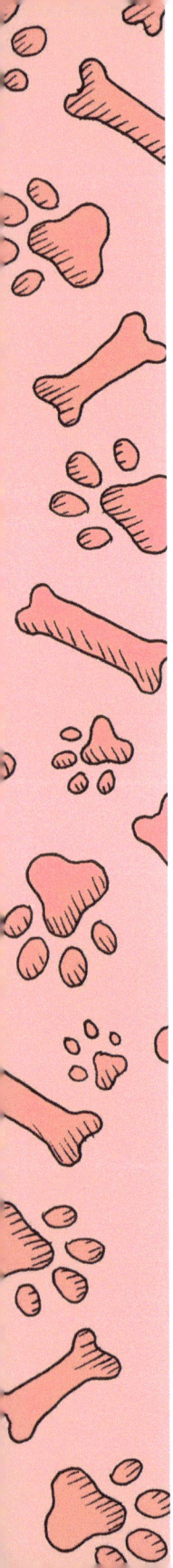

LOVING CARE

KARE
Kitsap Animal Rescue & Education

MAGGIE SPEAK., HER LEARNED VOCABULARY AND THE FOLLOWING STORIES ARE SHARED FROM THE VOLUNTEERS AT KARE. THEY WILL SHOW YOU JUST HOW LOVING CARE AND TRAINING CAN GIVE ANY DOG A NEW BEGINNING!

SHE HAS COME A LONG WAY THANKS TO THE VOLUNTEERS AT KARE.
TOP ROW: CATHY & DIANNE
BOTTOM ROW: UTA, CARLA, CHRIS AND HEIDI

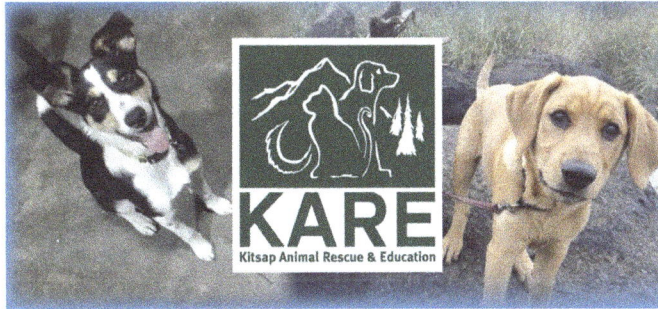

EDUCATE, ADVOCATE, REHABILITATE

KARE is an all-volunteer, non-profit organization providing animal welfare education and shelter rescue support. KARE's main focus is on helping people understand how to communicate with their pets in hopes of reducing the number of homeless pets in shelters. KARE also rescues adoptable dogs and cats that do not thrive in the shelter environment and simply need a good home, a little training, and love to make them great pets.

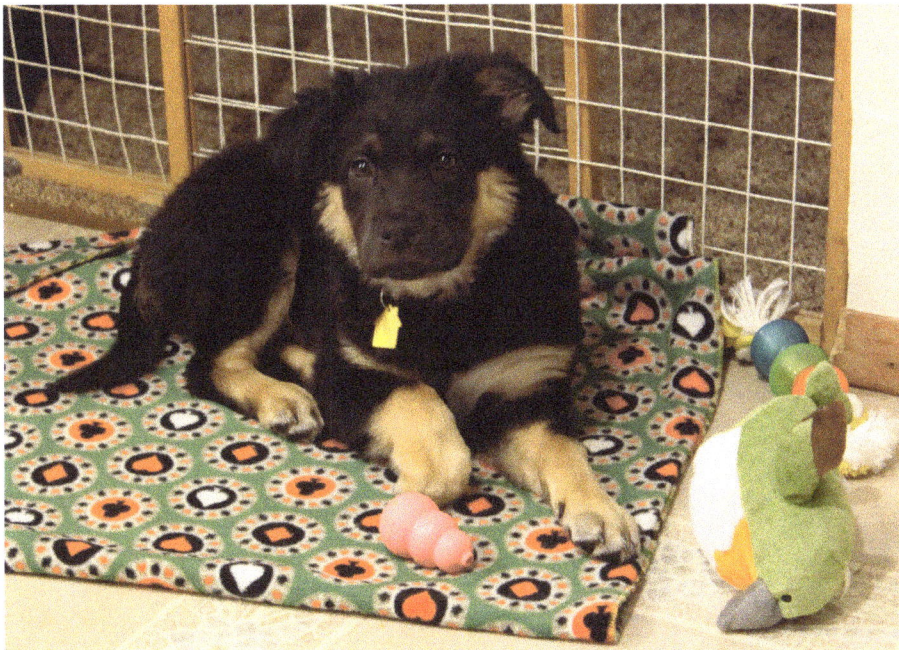

CARE TO KARE!

COULD ANIMALS RESCUE EVERYONE

KITSAP ANIMAL RESCUE AND EDUCATION

Uta Kramer, Co-Founder of KARE

Uta is fur addicted-loving, studying, training, and breathing the very thoughts of each dog she is in contact with making it her mission that no dog be cast away but trained so their lives are full and happy. Moving to the USA from Germany, she and her husband Kim had bought their home but they only completed the feeling of "home" after finding and taking in a furry stray making him part of their lives. That was the beginning of what turned out to be Uta's passion in life. Training dogs paying particulate attention to behavior. Learning and understand their behavior almost before it was visible and beginning a training path she used while working the next twenty two years at the Humane Society. Uta believed there was no attack without signs and she was determined to learn what those signs were in order to stop the attacks for both the love of the dogs and safety around them. Each of the next few dogs she added to their family aided in her passion for training.

Many trainers in our society are there for the income or they need a job but Uta loves every dog. She spends her time understanding and communicating with them-speaking doglish with them because she cares. If a dog has something to say, she listens and replies. Uta is a diamond amongst our dog world making sure they don't go without so in 2001 she began her journey into training so her life could make that difference in a dog's world. Her passion is evaluating dogs so she can understand what they need to improve their lives. Uta spent many years volunteering at the Humane Society so she could put her knowledge to good use making each dog a family member to others and saving their very breath in life. She does not see yellow, black, brown or any color but she sees them all as creatures to be loved and spoil -all equal and all worth saving. Uta is a blessing to all mankind, a friend to others and a true lover for dogs. Some people have best friends amongst their peers but I would say that Uta is likely happier to have a dog in her home than many people because they are loyal, forgiving. loving and never petty. Yes, Uta Kramer is our diamond in the sky, leading so many to that destination of happiness that in time, results in families united everywhere.

After our training at the KARE facility ended at the Humane Society, Uta Kramer volunteered to continue our traning while loving Maggie, becoming a close friend and our mentor. We had our foundation from them but now needed the care to be on going so as not to lose ground and continue to learn. Uta has been associated with KARE from the beginning and rescued many dogs herself with the vast knowledge and love she has for dogs-a natural for this style of life.

Maggie totally loves her and looks forward to visits to her home or from Uta visiting us at our home. Uta listens to us as well. We told her about an interest Maggie has with things that are related to agility and has brought to us suggestions and playthings that will aide in Maggie's training. She is a friend to Maggie and to us teaching us each day by example. She has also taught Maggie and us a new set of values. Maggie, although loving most people now, she is still not trusting of all dogs and this is where Uta comes in.

She was at the beginning of KARE's inception and remains in contact helping everywhere she can but now enjoys retirement as does her husband Kim. After years of sharing their love of the family dogs together with each Uta and Kim following their own dreams or hobbies, finally time has allowed them to play and work side by side through their retirement years. Perhaps we should tell you that a dedicated person such as Uta, never really retires so it was with her husband's dedication to her, much of what she does is both endorsed and embraced by him! No matter how busy, she makes time to help dogs in trouble.

Uta's first priority as we see it, are dogs with their well being and happiness at the forefront of her mind. Uta offers credits to her friends and colleagues as they, all credit one another for the growth in their world. We have to agree, as this is exactly how we feel giving each trainer credit for helping us in difficult time, trying to give our Maggie a chance in life. A quote from her is "The faces of happy dogs make me happy and my husband likes it too."

Merlin's Story by Uta Kramer

There he was, sitting in the corner of his shelter kennel and leaning against the wall. Afraid of every human who stood still and talked to him, even in a soft voice. He was scared to death of everything and everybody. Only when a dog with a person walked by that he looked at the dog.

There was a couple who took him for a walk every day for 6 weeks and every time he acted like he had never seen those people before, especially the man. He always moved away, no growling or biting. When he was outside he did not enjoy it. His tail flew under his belly and his body language was as if to say, "let me run away, everything looks scary to me." Poor thing. The owner had brought him into the shelter because he didn't have enough time for him. The dog had lived for 10 months in a crate almost 24 hours/day and now 2 month at the Shelter in his small kennel. No socialization at all, which is so important for a young dog. By now he was 1 year old, weighed 50 pounds, his fur was short and thick and he had the height of a husky. He was not a Husky/Sheppard mix? Or was he? It did not matter; he was wanted and could be fostered.

At the beginning he was a little shy but after two months my husband could pet him only under the table, so that their eyes did not meet. He became comfortable with me pretty soon because I fed him, took him for walks in quiet areas and played with him in our big backyard. He did not like guests in the house and always ran into the bedroom where his bed was/is. My husband and I decided to keep him because who wants a dog like that? There we were: failed foster. We named him Merlin because sometimes he still has that uncertain look in his eyes.

Today after 9 years he weighs 65 pounds, he is the best dog, but in Merlin's way. I can trust him with every dog, young or old, tall or small, he always treats them right. He warns the wild puppies with a growl and barks at them until they behave; and with the unfriendly dogs he just walks away and ignores them; no fighting. No fight, I always wanted a dog like that. He likes my husband but he loves me (I think). Of course we worked with him with other dogs and people. But he still is like young Merlin with strangers. He still avoids them always, is afraid, and does not want to get out of the car in town. We decided that's the way he is and will always be…so what! He is a happy go lucky dog on our property and on our walks through the fields. He likes to run with other dogs and accepted he was not to chase our llamas. We can't ever take him camping or on an airplane like our other dog but we never regret that we kept him. Merlin is Merlin—he is not our pet he is a member of our family.!!!!!! And we treat him as he needs it, with understanding and patience. No force in the world would have changed him and you cannot treat fear with harsh training. We love you Merlin.

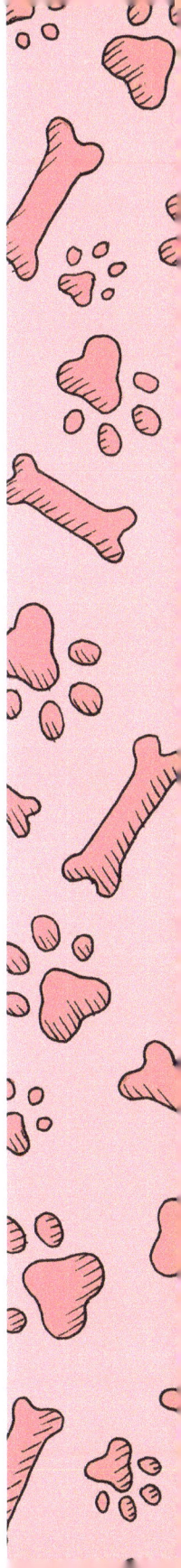

Dianne Canafax, Co-Founder of KARE

One of the original founding members of KARE is Dianne Canafax. Her goal is to educate people to know what fits their needs and successfully have a loving home for each family with their new furry friend. They offer training classes in subjects such as Doglish and behavioral mannerisms. Volunteers are like family to one another in shelters with one goal in mind, which is making lives enriched with the love of a great pet family member.

She is a trainer and teacher driven by her compassion to save the lives of so many dogs that her life may take her anywhere to find a dog to bring back for adoption.

Rufus, who is her Service Dog Assistant, began his journey in life in probably many ways we never truly want to know about and later lived in the shelter from the age of four months until he was ten months old. Rufus was passed up for adoption for six months due to his high levels of energy and undesirable behavior. But he was a puppy and was discovered by Dianne when she was preparing to teach a class…with one glance from him, he wrapped her around his little toes and it was instant love with this extraordinary dog! While she had a mission, so did Rufus. He looked at Dianne and spoke with his eyes, saying he wanted to please her and make her life better.

Adopting Rufus did not come without doubt from her husband and months of determination to help him learn even the smallest of lessons of even where to go potty, but he was so special Dianne just knew it was only time that he needed to feel safe and secure in his surroundings! It was a real problem but in time Rufus became that special Service Dog assistant for five years before retiring. He is now 13 years old and enjoying the good life.

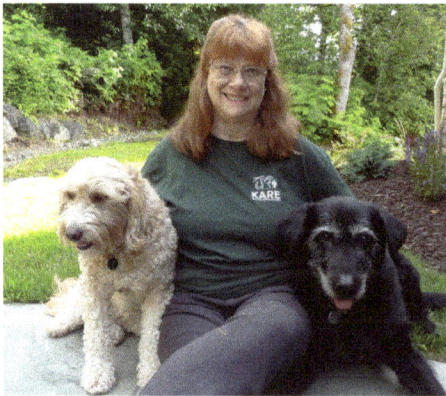

Dianne's exposure began decades ago with a best friend canine, Blackie. Her compassion as a child drove her to be a rescue person saving orphaned pheasants to strays of all kind. She was a puppy raiser for a national service dog agency. She learned that dogs could be happy family members if only trained which she found true in most of the dogs in shelters which then lead her to become obsessed with saving those lives.

When asking Dianne which dream in her life is the one closest to her heart, her reply was: "my greatest dream would be for KARE to grow to the point where we could build a behavior rehabilitation and training center."

Loving Carc

We personally got to know Dianne when she opened her arms to our family while we were so desperate to help our puppy Maggie get past her fear in life and her aggression towards us. Her outreach to us was the beginning of our happy home being united as a family. We joined her classes, volunteered where she needed us and worked with she and Cathy until we could go it alone but never let go of her caring of our Maggie and the well being of our family.

Now remember Maggie had come to us abused so she was in her mind, defending herself so not to be harmed again. Their Mission statement is: Educating people for the sake of their pets.

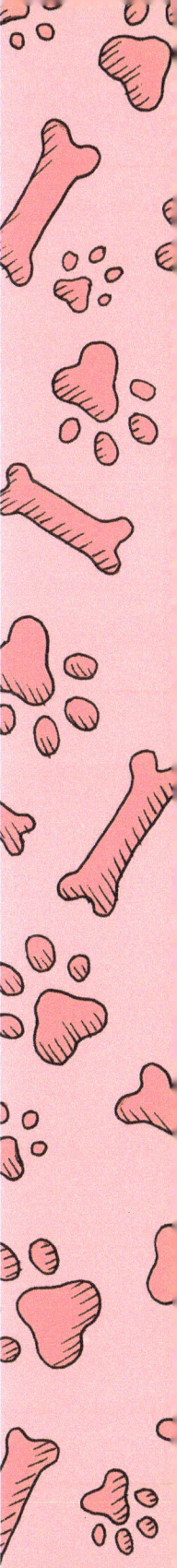

Cathy Hayes

One very special person that saved all of our lives and sanity was Cathy Hayes who is part of the originating team yet never was too busy not to pitch in and help our baby become what she is today. A fine and loving furry family member.

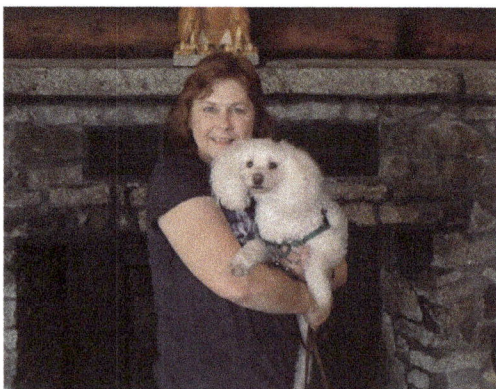

Here she is, Cathy Hayes with one of her rescue dogs, Skippy. We wish to thank Cathy publicly and tell all of you to reach out and call an agency nearest to you specializing in saving the lives of dogs. Work with that dedicated person who works with dogs in training, loving and re-homing each dog and one that follows up on each placement being sure these special dogs never know abuse again. Bravo to Cathy and all those that help to save the lives of these wonderful spirits and for us, especially Maggie Anne. Our family is complete with a dog that loves without fear and truly adores Cathy going nuts when she sees her in any crowd.

Cathy's career though she did not know at the time began when she was only 2 or 3 years of age. Today dogs are her passion but it began with a GORILLA! Yes, though she did not know at the time, this soft spoken and loving trainer began her journey at that age and though the gorilla so many years ago scared her so badly, today you will find a mellow and authoritative leader in training.

As a parent, the psychology one would think would be to assure Cathy to not be afraid because the gorilla was behind bars but not so here. To condition her, Cathy's parents lovingly took up dog training and with the largest breed they could find…Great Danes! They were naturals at it showing their dogs and even allowing Cathy to train a smaller dog of her own for show.

Loving Care

As a parent, the psychology one would think would be to assure Cathy to not be afraid because the gorilla was behind bars but not so here. To condition her, Cathy's parents lovingly took up dog training and with the largest breed they could find…Great Danes!

Cathy's parents made a wise choice selecting the largest dog they could find to rescue as the impact in her world would affect the rest of her life taking her on journey's most would only hope to travel. The Great Danes are known for their mellow temperaments and often referred to as the "sleeping giant" getting along well with people being reliable, trustworthy and dependable. So while the size of a gorilla may have startled or terrified Cathy, she learned through the love of her parent's size made no difference. It was the training and the knowledge of handling dogs that made the difference and a great beginning the rest of her life.

Cathy tells us a story about the first dog she trained when she was about ten years of age whose name was Teddybear. She lovingly trained her dog to do tricks and to sniff out mice! Oh, Teddybear did such a great job, he sniffed out the mice nestling in the family sofa which of course her obedient and studied dog immediately destroyed in order to expose her find! If not mistaken, Cathy found other ways to train her dog in the future not so expensive than furniture to replace! The end of that chapter in her life was that she was left being madly in love with dogs and excited with the capturing thought of one day becoming a trainer using the compassion born to her as a natural thanks to her parents and that gorilla.

She tells us that her other desire in life was to become a Veterinarian but the emotional side of seeing them injured or ill would have been too difficult so she joined the Humane Society in 2009 walking dogs in order to give them a time to be loved and out of their crates if only for a short time but it was enough to fuel Cathy's desire to continue learning everything she could absorb and where she met the instructor Dianne Canafax. She was also able to share her knowledge of Reiki so she shared it with the dogs too.

Although Cathy's profession was as an Accountant, in 2012 she was invited to join KARE and in spite of having such a busy life could not pass that opportunity up to fulfill her dreams. Soon she found that working accounting full time was no longer her lifestyle but dog training was so that is where one would find her most any day of a given day. Although she was raised in California with her parents that owned a business called Canadian Kennels where she was often surrounded by thirty dogs (most of which were Great Danes) we are lucky that her residence is

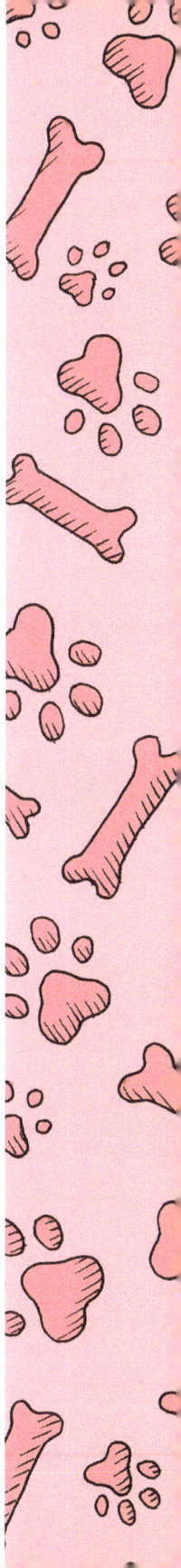

now in Washington State where the compassion was shared with our Maggie and so many others She says that if someone came to adopt a dog from her parents and the dogs did not like them, they did to get to take one figuring that while the dogs are smart they also had a better sense about people than humans did.

Today you will find Cathy most anytime working, training or searching for those special dogs that need her help. She also with her own dog Skippy reaches out to Hospice and nursing homes as he has a special way of knowing what patients need from him. Skippy has served as a Therapy Dog since 2012 and because of his generous loving manner she allows him to tell her what each patient needs. She says Skippy has never been wrong.

Heidi Wakefield

Meeting another of the board member is Heidi Wakefield whose love and determination shines with her attitude to bring the best out in each dog whose life she trains and loves making

sure each dog will always become a happier member of society than where they had come from as she also pushes forward to helping everywhere she can to build a strong organization.

Ace, now known as Kona by Heidi Wakefield

On 26 September 2007, Heidi met "Ace" a beautiful purebred Golden Retriever as he was being unloaded and processed by Animal Control in the truck bay at the Kitsap Humane Society.

He had been surrendered by his owner due to terrorizing the neighborhood and he was not a happy camper! Ace, now known as Kona, barked and glared at anyone who dare walk past his kennel. None of the volunteers wanted to walk him so I decided to stop each way to work and home to take him for his daily walks. I was so in love with this sweet and beautiful dog wanting him to be happy but the Humane Society had ruled he was not safe to adopt due to his behavior. I so agonized about his impending fate of being put down so I convinced the powers to be into letting me take Ace home in order to see if he would get along with our other furry family members.

Loving Care

Now, this dog was very smart and crawled into Scott's lap, (my husband) and made himself at home getting along with everyone with no problems! So the two of us decided Ace was there to stay. We proceeded to adopt him.

Oh, the dreaded day arrived…Day 21 and Ace put out his true colors for all to see attacking the neighbors Bouviers and became aggressive to all visitors to our home. Fortunately I knew Uta Kramer, a dog trainer and a long process of special traning began on a daily basis.

I ask Uta how long this steady training would go on Uta replied to me it could take up to one year and I remembered feeling overwhelmed and defeated when she me that it might take a year to get him turned around and exasperated I replied "A year? Could we possibly live with this a year?" We had our hands full but determined and convinced Ace would make a great pal, we refused to ever give up.

Installing a big fence around our property, training and rehabilitation occurred every day, all day so Ace would become that treasured family member we knew he could be. With both Scott and I receiving positive reinforcement from Uta, the now Kona had changed into a wonderful dog. Now after eight years he has his safe boundaries, which had some limitations and protection issues, but greets people with a big tail wag and a toy in his mouth.

We are finally a happy family again with Scott and Kona becoming the best of friends. Imagine seeing Kona sitting in the passenger seat of a Corvette as Scott takes her for their rides or the two of them at the end of dock fishing and you will also see a very happy dog!

Scott and I say that Kona lives because of KARE training, rehabilitation, and love. Uta, the dog trainer, told me, "The dogs that take the most work are the ones that capture your heart."

Carla Peterson, Tireless Volunteer

When we began as a volunteer at the Humane Society, we met Carla Peterson who is dedicated to being sure each dog was walked, fed, played with and given some special treat she herself very often made but most of all, loved. Carla not only saw to the dogs being treated but you would usually find cookies or some special goodie she brought to treat the volunteers she led.

She became our mentor and our leader, with each day as a volunteer we found her even more patient and knowable than the week before. Carla was always willing to help another

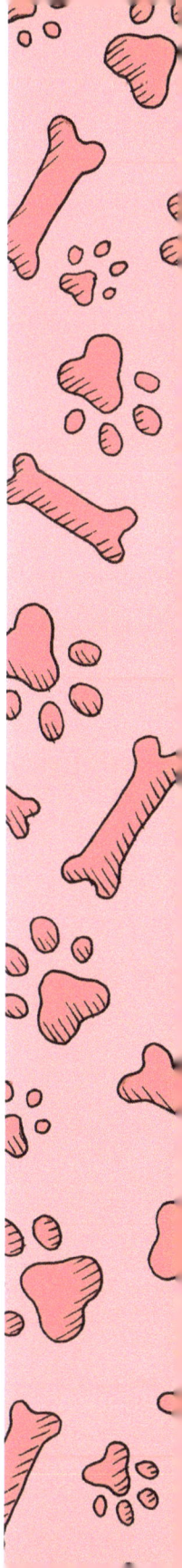

volunteer be the best they could be. After all, the dogs were to benefit so perfection is what you could expect to find. After we adopted Maggie Anne, she and her sweetheart, Chris spent time with us helping make Maggie some of her first homemade cookies. The two of them are a perfect match as they share the compassion of being sure dogs are loved and trained with only positive reinforcements carefully and to avoid the training some use with fear tactics.

Carla worked endless hours as a volunteer after a full time job and had a dog of her own with special needs but Chris always covered the home base caring for Amos so Carla could continue working with so many other dogs in need. Her dedication truly paid off with finding dogs new forever homes and after years of exhausting schedules, she jumped in to another organization. KARE was her new direction to volunteer with whatever jobs needed to be done leading them to victor on several occasions. Knowing Carla, you have to wonder where she finds such endless energy but helping anyone when it comes to issues surrounding dogs, she will always rebound for the dogs in her life.

She was instrumental in setting up the social media on Facebook and it took off while she was also working tirelessly in finding new ways to raise funds with fundraisers. Carla is a powerhouse of enthusiasm that gets the job done but her first priority is to be sure each dog she knows about is safe and happy. Many people have cause to thank her and from our viewpoint, she is a great friend and colleague. Our family has enjoyed the opportunity of getting to know her better

Here is Carla's salute to her very own rescue dog-Amos!

I bought Amos from a pet store in October 2002 giving into my sister's persistence that I needed a dog now that I finished graduate school and had my first full time job. He was sold to me as a Dachshund/Beagle mix which later turned out to not be true. He was 6 pounds at 3 months old. I'm pretty sure I got a backyard breeder or puppy mill dog. Amos has a fear of handling.

Amos is the first dog that I've had on my own. We went through several training classes and he did well. He traveled with me to Honolulu, Hawaii in early 2004 for work.

Later in 2004, I took Amos to Washington, DC with me for work. I'm not sure when his handling fear got so bad, but in March 2005; he was attacked by a St. Bernard in heat. He received a large puncture wound in his shoulder. I had a work conference that I couldn't cancel so I left him at Olympic Animal Hospital for his care. He did not do well there and his handling fear seems to have become worse since then.

Over time, Amos came to tolerate some petting and I can now massage certain areas to check his lumps and bumps. That in itself has taken over 10 years of work. I've also learned to manage his fear and also use positive reinforcement to train new behaviors.

I also found Kitsap Animal Rescue and Education and become involved with them as well. Volunteering with KARE and Kitsap Humane Society has increase my dog behavior knowledge, training, and handling skills. It's also helped improve my relationship with Amos.

Amos loves to play fetch and swim! He loves to play and work his mind doing puzzles and food dispensing toys. He also likes to cuddle and be near me. We've found that we are quite bonded together after being together for 12 years. He is such a character and he makes me laugh and I can't help but smile when I see his face. Through all the blood, sweat, and tears (literally), I've never given up on Amos. He is by far the most challenging dog that I've had. Well, he's also my first dog on my own. Amos has taught me a lot about life and dogs. He is the reason I'm so interested in helping dogs stay out of the shelter. Amos is my best buddy and dog. I love him more than anything in this world. I hope to have many more years with my best friend.

Maggie Speak!

by

Rosemary "Mamie" Adkins

We're so proud of our girl! Even though she was just a sweet little baby when we first adopted her, we feared she may never overcome the extreme abuse she suffered in her first few weeks of life *(see her full story in this book)*. It took some doing on our part, but we're proud to say that love and trust have won her heart and she is thriving in more ways than we ever dreamed of.

Today, our Maggie is a happy, bouncing little girl with an impressive vocabulary that continues to grow every day. We have always communicated in every way we could imagine in order to stimulate her recovery and development. Maggie learned to respond to and trust our loving touch, softly spoken words and the assurance that she would wake up every day to our familiar presence.

So we had an idea! Why not list our Maggie-words and phrases and watch it grow as she matures. <u>You should try it</u>! Your furry little friends just might astound you with their development and intellect. Here is Maggie's, at the time of writing this book, of all the words and phrases that Maggie understands when we speak them to her.

Words		
Angel	dishwasher	playpen
baby	door	playtime
ball	down	Ride
beef-heart	freezer	sit
blackie	hug	squirrel
bone	Icy	stay
boo boo	laundry	TV
car	marshmallow	up (onto lap)
come	no	vacuum

Loving Care

Words		
cookie	outside	walk
cross (street)	Oven	Yum
dinner	pillow	
Phrases		
cross the street	go to bed	pretty girl
drop it	good girl	see Daddy
get Daddy	leave it	see Mommie
get Mommie	let's get the mail	time for bath
get your toes	let's go	want to pay ball
give me a hug	let's go to bed	want to watch TV
give me a kiss	nite nite	where's our beautiful girl
dinner	pillow	
Names		
Daddy	Martha	Sara
Heather	Mommie	Tony
Linda	Pixie	
Loki	Santa	
Toys		
ball	Burro	Pickle
Blackie	Mr. Greenie	
Buddy	Mrs. Scarlett	

APPENDIXES

- Nutritional Benefits of the Main Ingredients
- Ingredients You Need to Avoid
- Ingredient Substitutions
- Seasonings Safe for Dogs
- First Aid

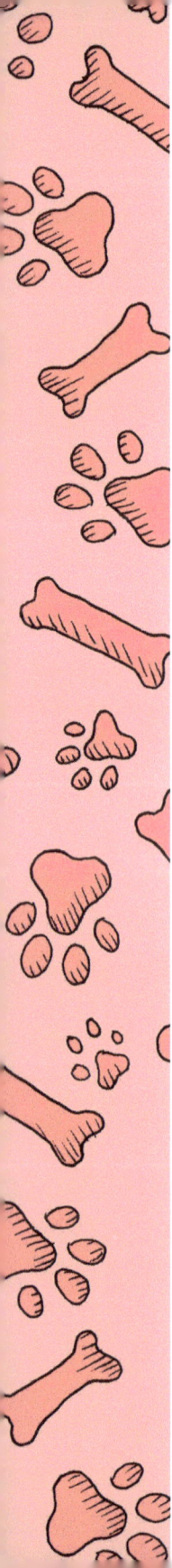

APPENDIX A:

Nutritional Benefits of the Main Ingredients in our Dog Food Recipes

The following is a list of the benefits for dogs of the main ingredients we use in our delicious dog food recipes. These values are determined for organic foods and we highly advise cooking with organics for the health of your dog. All the dog treat recipes in *Maggie's Kitchen Tails* use human grade food ingredients because we feel that our pets deserve the very best. Be sure and go over this list with your own vet to make sure each of these ingredients is good for your particular dog. Many dogs have allergies to various food items, but you can always make a healthy ingredient substitution (more on substitutions in Appendix C).

The information in Appendix A and B is cross-referenced from a number of websites with information from experts on dog nutrition including:

- https://www.aspca.org/pet-care/pet-nutrition-service (the American Society for Prevention of Cruelty to Animals),
- http://vetmedicine.about.com
- http://www.woofstop.com/ingredients.html and http://pets.thenest.com.)

Meat (cooked) and Fish

<u>Chicken</u> is packed with protein for the building blocks of life for your dog, phosphorus for your dog's healthy bones and teeth, and B-Complex for healthy blood vessels.

<u>Beef</u> is high in protein and phosphorus (once cooked) with some needed calcium for dogs.

<u>Turkey</u> is also high in protein and one of the highest meats in calcium and phosphorus.

<u>Salmon</u> is one of the best fish for your dog and is high in omega 3 fatty acids; good for dog's coat and immune system. You may also use tuna, sardines, mackerel, herring, anchovies, trout and catfish for ingredients in your dog food.

Veggies

<u>Bell Peppers</u> provide beta carotene and fiber, as well as anti-oxidants.

<u>Carrots</u> contain beta carotene/vitamin A, high fiber, and are good for dog's teeth.

<u>Celery</u> is excellent for dogs

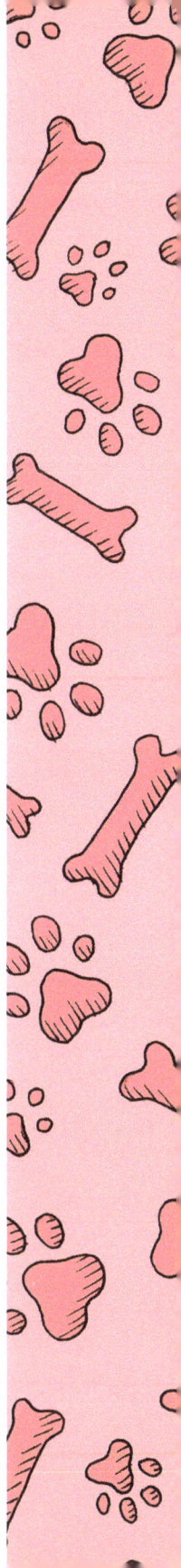

<u>Collards</u> are rich in vitamin C and Vitamin A, and are high in fiber, supporting your dog's digestive system.

<u>Garbanzo beans and flour (Chickpea)</u> are high in protein and make an excellent partial flour substitution for grains. It is an easily digestible protein and is an excellent source of folic acid, potassium and fiber, in addition to being a good source of iron, magnesium, copper, zinc and phosphorus. Chickpeas also contain thiamine, niacin, vitamin B6 and calcium.

<u>Green Beans</u> are high in vitamins A, K and C, magnesium and fiber. Vitamin A, a fat-soluble vitamin, helps to preserve your dog's eye health and maintain optimal heart health.

<u>Idaho potatoes</u> are healthy in small amounts for your dog. You may even wish to use mashed potatoes as an icing on a dog cake.

<u>Peas and Pea Flour</u> contains high amounts of a health-protective polyphenol called coumestrol and has high fiber and protein.

<u>Pumpkin</u> (pure without added sugar or other ingredients) is high in fiber, beta-carotene/vitamin A and are full of C, Iron. The fiber can be very helpful in the maintenance of digestive health of your dog.

<u>Spinach</u> is powerhouse for iron, as well as supplying calcium, potassium and various antioxidants.

<u>Sweet Potatoes</u> are high in fiber, high in Vitamin B6, Vitamin C, Vitamin A/beta carotene, fiber, potassium, iron, copper and manganese.

<u>Tomatoes</u> are high in antioxidants, which help nourish the body with Vitamin A (carontnoids), lycopene, quercitin, and Vitamin C.

<u>Zucchini</u> is high in potassium, Vitamin A and C, and are rich in flavonoid poly-phenolic antioxidants such as carotenes, lutein and zea-xanthin.

Fruit

<u>Apples and applesauce</u> (cored, no seeds) contain calcium, vitamin K, vitamin C, and pectin (which is a soluble fiber), and are good for dog's breath.

<u>Blueberries</u> contain photochemicals that benefit the immune system in dogs. They contain fiber, vitamin K, manganese, and some studies have found that they help to reduce stroke damage in

pets and heart disease. Blueberries are rich in natural antioxidants that play an important role in preventing an increase of oxidative damage in senior dogs.

Bananas are rich in potassium (essential for maintaining an optimal fluid balance in your dog's body) and vitamin C, which helps in boosting your dog's immune system.

Cranberries are rich in vitamins including A, B1, B2, and C. They also are full of minerals and antioxidants and are an excellent supplement to your dog's diet for the promotion of urinary tract health.

Strawberries have antioxidants and high fiber with lots of vitamin C, and contain an enzyme to help whiten dog's teeth.

Herbs

Cinnamon is good for dogs with painful joints due to arthritis because of its anti-inflammatory properties that reduce the stiffness and help ease the pain of this musculoskeletal disorder. Its calcium and fiber content is effective in fighting heart diseases. It has antifungal and antibacterial properties and thus it may be helpful in dealing with external and internal infections. Remember that most cinnamon obtained in USA is not Ceylon Cinnamon and it really related to the pea family. If your dog is allergic to peas, consult your vet before using.

Garlic has many benefits for dogs including: high in calcium, zinc, potassium, Vitamin A, B, B2 and C. It is also a natural dog flea repellent and de-wormer. It has trace amounts of thiosulphate, which can cause anemia in dogs if eaten in larger amounts (as in onions, which are much higher in thiosulphate). We suggest garlic in reasonable amounts because it has such high benefits.

Ground Ginger is an anti-coagulant, anti-inflammatory, an antibacterial. Ginger also helps in the absorption of food and helps boost healthy blood circulation. Good for your dog's digestion and teeth.

Mint is excellent for freshening your dog's breath. The only species of mint, in the genus Mentha, that is toxic to dogs, is English pennyroyal (Mentha pulegium).

Parsley is a powerful herb that contains high levels of Vitamin A/beta carotene, vitamin B12, chlorophyll, calcium, and is fortified with vitamin C. It aids in digestion, liver support, kidneys, and adrenal glands, purifies blood and bodily fluids and helps boost your dog's immune system. Also good for your dog's breath.

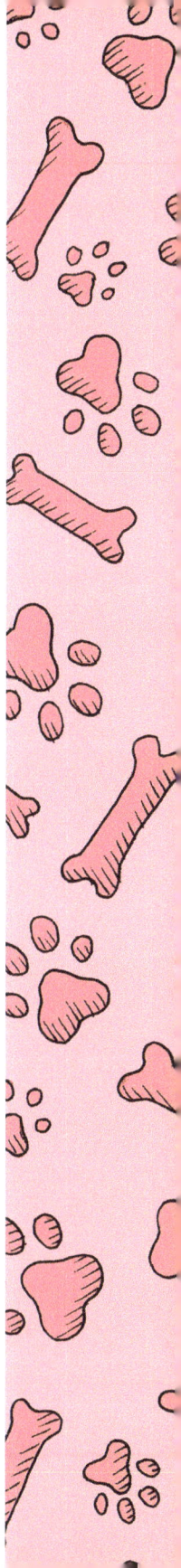

Rosemary is high in fiber, is an anti-oxidant and an anti-inflammatory. Also has an anti-fungal property.

Turmeric is a powerful anti-inflammatory and great for arthritic dogs. It has beneficial qualities for most dogs.

Nuts

Almonds and almond flour is high in protein and also makes an excellent flour substitution in treats.

Peanut Butter (all natural brands) contains protein, healthy fats, vitamin B, and vitamin E, which benefits a dog's coat and immune system. It contains omega-3 and thus may help extended the lifespan of your dog, reduced inflammation from arthritis, and improve heart health. Some dogs are allergic to peanuts.

Grains

(Some experts in dog nutrition agree that dogs do not need grains in their diet. However other experts suggest that whole grains can add nutrition that is not found in vegetables or meat and is valuable in a dog's diet in small quantities (it is important to use whole grains rather than white flours). Be sure and assess which grains your dog can tolerate and to which they do not have allergies. We have known dogs that could tolerate whole wheat and oats but not barley or rice. And the reverse may also be true.

Barley is high in fiber and can make an excellent flour substitution for dogs allergic to wheat.

Brown Rice is easily digestible and is high in fiber and a great source of manganese, magnesium and selenium. Brown rice is rich in antioxidants and promotes weight loss and may help to stabilize blood sugar levels.

Millet is a good source of vitamin B for your dog and high in fiber. Millet should not be fed to dogs with thyroid issues due to its thyroid inhibiting properties.

Oatmeal (wholegrain) and (Rolled) Oat flour is high in soluble fiber, and is good for keeping bowels regular (which is helpful for senior dogs). You can now buy gluten-free oats if your dog is known to have a gluten allergy.

Quinoa is gluten-free and high in both protein and vitamin B-12.

Whole Wheat contains ample amounts of vitamin B.

Other Ingredients:

<u>Organic Agave</u> is thought to be okay for dogs in very small amounts in an occasional treat. It does have some anti-oxide benefits.

<u>Buckwheat Flour</u> is not a wheat, not a grain but is a berry. Dogs with grain allergies may be safe to eat treats containing Buckwheat. Buckwheat contains magnesium, which improves the cardiovascular system.

<u>Coconut, Coconut Oil, and Coconut Flour</u> all can be used as ingredients in dog food, but be aware that it could be too rich for a puppy. The health benefits are

<u>Corn and Cornmeal</u> is not highly digestible for dogs nor is it high in nutritional value and thus should be used sparingly. Some dogs can tolerate it, but it is not advisable to use it except sparingly.

<u>Eggs</u> (whole cooked) is high in protein, riboflavin and selenium.

<u>Flax Seed</u> (ground) is high in omega-3 fatty acids, and is good for dog's skin and coat. It is high in anti-oxidants, nutrients, minerals and vitamins that are essential for optimal health of your dog.

<u>Filtered water</u> is best to use for a healthy pooch as tap water may not be 100% safe.

<u>Honey</u> is full of vitamins and minerals like vitamin B6, thiamin, niacin, riboflavin calcium, copper, iron, magnesium, manganese, phosphorous, potassium, sodium and zinc.

<u>Maple Syrup</u> is okay for dogs in very small amount unless they are diabetic.

<u>Olive Oil</u> is high in omega-3 and may lessen the effects of cardiovascular disease in your dog. It also contains oleic acid, in addition to some compounds (squalene and terpenoids) that are believed to be effective in preventing cancer. It is also high in vitamin E, chlorophyll, and carotenoids.

<u>Yogurt</u> (without added sugar or sweeteners, low-fat Greek) is high in protein and in calcium, and contains probiotics that are good for dog's digestion.

<u>Unsulphured Black Strap Molasses</u> is the healthiest form of molasses for your dog. It contains iron, folate and B vitamins for healthy red blood cell production, magnesium and calcium for healthy bones and nervous system and a healthy heart, manganese that stabilizes blood sugar and utilizes fatty acids and copper and zinc.

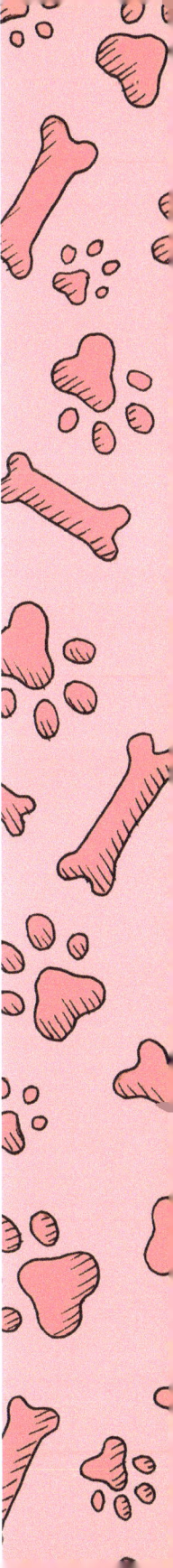

APPENDIX B:
Ingredients You Need to Avoid or Use with Caution in Dog Food

<u>Avocados</u> contain persen and while not harmful to humans it is toxic to many dogs.

<u>Onions</u>—raw or cooked— can destroy a dog's red blood cells and lead to anemia. It contains a large amount of thiosulphate, which is known to cause the Heinx Factor or anemia in dogs.

<u>Grapes and Raisons</u> have been known to be highly toxic to dogs causing kidney failure (even in very small amounts).

<u>Dairy products</u> (milk) can cause diarrhea in dogs.

<u>Macadamia nuts</u> can be fatal for dogs so completely avoid!

<u>No chocolate, alcohol, candy, sodas, cane sugar, comfrey, pepper, and no added salt to food.</u>

<u>Apple seeds, apricot pits, cherry pits and peach pits</u> are all toxic to dogs, although the fruit is okay.

APPENDIX C
Ingredient Substitutions

We have used a variety of grains in our dog food recipes that are good for dogs and many increase the protein and other nutritional value of these baked goods. Here are some ideas for you in using alterative nutritious flours other than wheat to be substituted for part or all of the wheat flour often called for in a recipe:

1. <u>Quinoa</u> flour is highly nutritious with more protein, calcium and iron than most other grain flours. It has a nice nutty taste, so it is best used in small amounts in a recipe.

2. <u>Kamut</u>® is an ancient type of wheat related to the modernly used durum variety. Compared to regular whole wheat, Kamut® is richer in protein, vitamins, minerals, and unsaturated fatty acids. While this is good for dogs, the down side is that it contains a little less dietary fiber. Kamut® flour has a mild and rather sweet taste. It can be substituted cup for cup for whole wheat in baking.

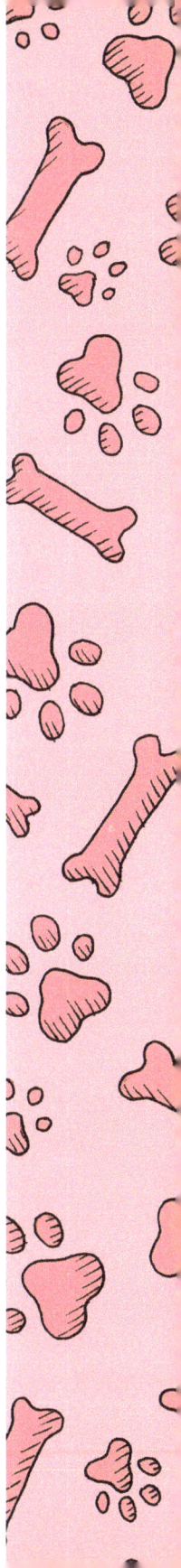

3. <u>Buckwheat flour</u> is considered gluten-free. It has a robust flavor. We often substitute a cup of buckwheat for 1 cup of wheat flour in our recipes, but we always use an abundance of additional ingredients for flavor as buckwheat can take over the taste of the baked good.

4. <u>Millet flour</u> is ground from millet seeds and is gluten-free with a buttery, sweet taste. It is high in vitamins and minerals. But because it can be a little grainy, only use a small amount in each recipe (in other words, a little goes a long way).

5. <u>Amaranth flour</u> is gluten-free and can be substituted cup for cup in a whole wheat recipe and teams well with buckwheat flour.

6. <u>Coconut flour</u> is very high in fiber. It is low in carbohydrates and a high in protein. It gives baked goods a rich flavor but it needs a lot more liquid than other flours so be sure and add extra water to a recipe if you use it for substitutions. Coconut flour has a natural sweet taste.

7. <u>Oat Flour</u> is an excellent source of fiber and adds a rich sweetness to your homemade dog treats. Bob's Red Mill has recently added certified gluten-free oats to its line of gluten-free products. I like to grind my own, using organic rolled oats in a coffee grinder, and find it can be substituted for at least half of the flour in a recipe calling for wheat. We love to use it in our dog treats because oats help make the dough roll out and shape into cookies and biscuits so easily.

(The information in Appendix C is contributed from Martha Char Love's cookbook Mom's Island Bakens: Over 50 Altered Recipes for a Happy Gut and a Health Heart.)

APPENDIX D
Seasonings Safe for your Dog

Aloe Vera
Barley
Basil
Caraway Seeds
Celery Root Extract
Cinnamon
Fennel Seeds
Flax Seeds

Ginger

Green Tea

Lentils

Malted Barley

Parsley

Rooibos Tea

Rosemary

Sage

Sea Salt

Sorbic Acid-used for preservatives

Sunflower Oil

Turmeric

Some of our facts here were provided and found on the Internet by: Dog Foods Naturally: http://www.dogshealthnaturally.com and http://www.tarquins-pet-friendly.com

We have researched safe herbs and spices safe to use when you are preparing your own dog treats and meals.

We have done so in an attempt to help you spice up safely the foods your dog eats that add not only flavor but also nutrients for the overall well being of dog. Please when you buy herbs use the organic so they are without the pesticides commonly used on produce, herbs and general vegetation while being raised. We try to raise our own but the ones we don't, we purchase. Some won't do well over different seasons but we purchased a dehydrator for that purpose so that even if using dried they are still free from those chemicals.

Safety is what we have stressed in our book. Here again, we recommend that before you use any seasonings, herbs, spices or you are unsure of them, consult your Veterinarian for any possible side effects.

Alfalfa is rich in calcium, copper, folate, iron, magnesium, manganese, phosphorous, potassium, silicon and zinc, vitamins A, B1, B12, C, D, E, and K. It is also an antioxidant used to reduce pain and swelling associated with arthritis, nutritive (good for bone building) and a diuretic.

Anise seed has anti-oxidant, disease preventing and many health promoting properties. Anise is rich in B Complex Vitamins, Vitamin A and C (anti-oxidants) and important minerals such as copper, iron, magnesium, manganese zinc and potassium.

Basil is a very good source of vitamin A, but also helps prevent free radicals from oxidizing cholesterol in the blood stream. Only after it has been oxidized does cholesterol build up in blood vessel walls, initiating the development of atherosclerosis, whose end result can be a heart attack or stroke. It is also a good source of **magnesium**, which promotes cardiovascular health by prompting muscles and blood vessels to relax, thus improving blood flow and lessening the risk of irregular heart rhythms or a spasming of the heart muscle or a blood vessel. This information provided by: whfoods.org-the Worlds Healthiest Foods.

Carob is low in fat and sodium, high in fiber, potassium, and calcium, and can improve digestion. It has a natural sweetness and contains very little fat, no caffeine and encourages the absorption of calcium. Even though carob looks like, chocolate, it does not contain theobromine, the part of chocolate that is toxic to dogs.

Caraway Seeds are rich in dietary fiber, vital vitamins, and minerals, anti-oxidants (cancer and disease fighting). Caraway seeds are considered a warming herb meaning they help the body stay warm. Caraway seeds are also good for muscle health (anti-contraction), help prevent constipation, and remove a large amount of harmful toxins from the body which helps prevent some cancers.

Catnip is not just for cats. It contains Magnesium, manganese, flavonoids, tannins, vitamins C and E, and essential oils such as neroli, citronellol, nepetalactone, and thymol. It has a mild tranquilizing effect on most animals so is effective for treating restlessness, nervousness, and insomnia. The gas relieving and antispasmodic effect of catnip also makes it excellent for treatment of flatulence, diarrhea, and dyspepsia, and is effective in treating early symptoms of colds, flu's, and especially bronchitis. Tip-put some fresh leaves in drinking water or sprinkle the dried herb (1/8 to 1/2 teaspoon of per pound of food) on a meal.

Cayenne Pepper is a hot and spicy source of vitamin A, vitamin E, vitamin C, vitamin B6, fiber, vitamin K, manganese, and dietary fiber. It is the only pepper considered to be safe for dogs. All others should never be used so for this reason in spite of its usefulness, we never use this pepper.

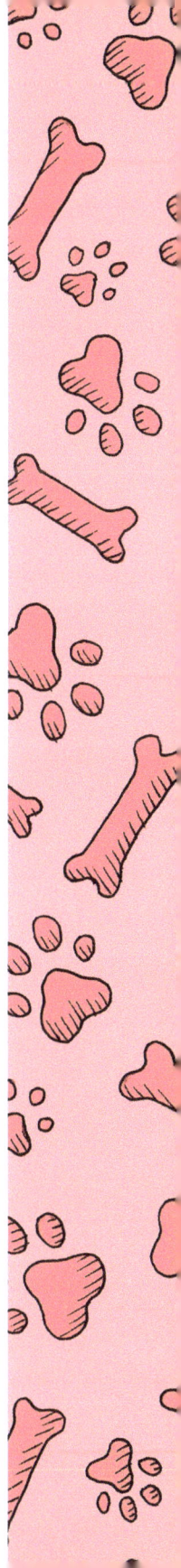

Chamomile as for human as well can be used as a sedative to alleviate anxiety and insomnia. The herb tea or tincture is useful for indigestion, gas, and vomiting. Its calming property is particularly helpful for cases of indigestive upset resulting from anxiety, nervousness and hyperactivity. This is one of the safest herbs; some dogs are allergic to the plant so check for sensitivity first before applying it to your dog. Also limit the use of this herb on pregnant dogs.

Chia Seeds contain large quantities of protein, five times the calcium of milk, boron (a trace mineral that aids in the absorption of calcium into the bones), Omega oils 3 and 6, and can help regulate blood sugar levels and aid in maintaining a healthy weight. The seeds of chia plants can help maintain healthy cholesterol levels and blood pressure, and reduce risk of heart disease. These seeds have no discernible odor and almost no taste, which means they can be added to your dog's meals without altering the flavors they love. Seeds can be ground, eaten raw, or added to water, which will cause the seeds to produce what is called chia seed gel. This gel helps clean out intestines and slows digestion, allowing your dog's body to absorb more of the incredible nutrients that chia seeds provide.

Cilantro (Corriander) is considered a digestive aid since it acts mainly on the digestive system, moderating the secretion of gastric juices and stimulating the appetite. It relieves gas and indigestion.

Cinnamon (Ceylon) is recommended to relieve vomiting and aid digestion. Cinnamon is said to have one of the highest anti-oxidant levels of all food source. Cinnamon is good for keeping teeth clean and fighting bad breath. According to the Wall Street Journal, you should be using Ceylon cinnamon, which is a milder form of the spice sold in gourmet stores, because it is healthier than ordinary supermarket cinnamon. Cinnamon can lower blood sugar in diabetics, ease arthritis and improve cholesterol.

Dandelion contains vitamins A, C, D, E, K, B complex, potassium, calcium, iron, thiamin, choline, lecithin, and riboflavin. This herb is also a strong but safe diuretic and liver stimulant, and it is rich supply of potassium. It also increases bile flow to the gallbladder which proves to be helpful for dogs suffering from liver congestion, gallstones, and other forms of liver problems.

Dill improves appetite, digestion and flatulence. It eases bloating due to gas and improves the digestive process because the gut gets better at extracting nutrients from foods and fewer nutrients are lost in excrement.

Fennel is crunchy and slightly contains protein, Vitamin A, Vitamin C, niacin, calcium, iron, magnesium, phosphorous, potassium, zinc, copper, and Omega-6 fatty acids. It acts as a detoxifier and strong digestive aid.

Fennel Seeds are used mainly as a digestive and have been known to normalize the appetite and aid weight loss. They also treat flatulence, calm the digestive tract, cleanse the liver, helpful with detoxifying the body as a whole, and are a natural diuretic.

Flaxseed, known as linseeds, plays a significant role in canine cardiovascular health and skin and coat health since it is an important source of fiber and antioxidants, and it may have anti-tumor properties as well. Omega-3 fatty acid and B vitamins, and ground flaxseed may be added in place of oils in the diet. It not only improves the shine of the pet's coat but aids in the movement of food through the digestive system.

Garlic contains germanium - an anti-cancer agent, helps to regulate blood pressure, helps strengthen the body's defenses against allergies, and regulate blood sugar levels. It's considered an aid to fighting and treating diabetes and liver, heart and kidney disease. It provides Vitamin A, B, B2, C, Calcium, Potassium, and Zinc. Garlic is a natural flea repellent and de-wormer. Garlic is listed under Foods That Harm Dogs because large amounts given over a prolonged period can result in the formation of Heinz bodies on the surface of red blood cells which are then destroyed by the body resulting in a severe hemolytic anemia. Whole Dog Journal claims a healthy dog can tolerate 1 clove per 20 pounds of body weight per day without any toxic effects.

Ginger is an antioxidant and anti-inflammatory used to treat digestive upset, nausea, gas, motion sickness, heart problems, joint inflammation due to arthritic conditions, to reduce fever, and is also effective as an anti-infective, especially against viruses. It can decrease blood sugar levels, and increase absorption of all oral medications. Too much ginger may cause nausea, especially when given on an empty stomach, and can affect how well blood clots. Do not give to a dog with a gastric ulcer or pregnant dogs.

Green Tea is rich in anti-oxidants and calming. It contains catechins which are more powerful than vitamins C and E in halting oxidative damage to cells and provide a reduced risk for heart disease and several cancers such as skin, breast, lung, colon, esophageal, and bladder. Make sure you only use de-caffeinated green tea.

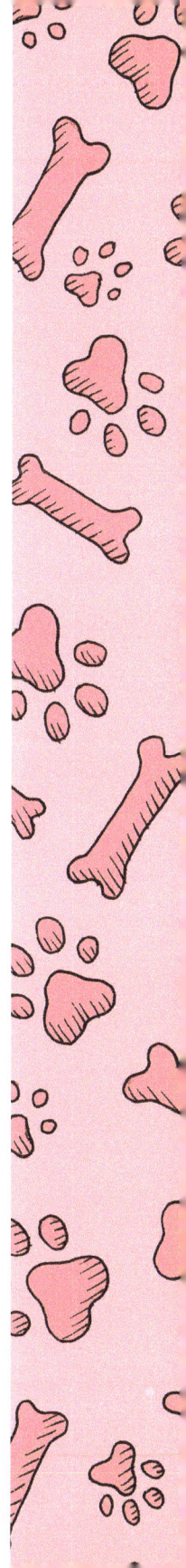

Kelp (seaweed) is a nutritional powerhouse containing Vitamin A, Vitamin C, Vitamin E, Vitamin K, folate, iodine, calcium, iron, magnesium, phosphorous, potassium, zinc, copper, manganese and selenium. Kelp benefits thyroid function, promotes heart health, helps fight and prevent cancer, is a powerful anti-oxidant, aids in healing skin disorders and enhancing coat health. It can be purchased in dried form at most health stores.

Licorice is an effective anti-inflammatory, due to the presence of Glycyrrhizin, which has a similar chemical structure to that of natural corticosteroids released by the adrenal glands. Glycyrrhizin stimulates the adrenals and is useful for treating Addison's disease. The herb also acts on the digestive system by promoting cell growth and alleviating ulcers and is also beneficial in treating liver toxicity. For the upper respiratory tracts, licorice root has long been used to alleviate coughs and ease discomfort brought on by bronchitis due to its demulcent, anti-inflammatory, and expectorant properties. To treat or prevent any of the above ailments, the best way is to feed your dog tinctures of the herb. Licorice can raise sugar levels in blood and should be used with caution in diabetic dogs. Do not use licorice for dogs with heart disease.

Milk Thistle is well known as a "liver herb" both for humans and pets. It contains a flavonoid compound called "silymarin" which itself is a combination of several other active compounds. Extensive studies around the world have found that silymarin is safe and effective in treating a variety of liver diseases and other conditions, from kidney disease to mushroom or lead poisoning. It works by displacing toxins trying to bind to the liver and by causing the liver to regenerate more quickly. In addition, silymarin can work as an antioxidant for the liver - it scavenges free radicals and stabilizes liver cell membranes. It also stimulates the production of new liver cells. Holistic veterinarians (and some conventional ones as well) have long been using milk thistle to treat dog liver disease. It has an excellent safety record and no known adverse drug interactions, although taking too much of the herb at a time can sometimes cause an upset stomach, gas, or mild diarrhea.

Oregano is a rich natural source of fiber and Omega-3 fatty acids. It contains Vitamin K, anti-oxidants, iron, manganese, fiber, and is a natural source of Omega-3 fatty acids. It is renowned for its anti-bacterial, anti-viral, anti-fungal and anti-parasitic properties.

Parsley Leaves are packed with B vitamins, C vitamins, carotene, iron and calcium. In addition to its use for dog bad breath, it can stimulate the kidneys to filter out toxins and increase urine.

Peppermint is known for its soothing effect of an upset stomach, respiratory infections, viral infections and skin conditions. It provides effective relief of flatulence and indigestion. Its anti-parasitic medical properties are an alternate solution in the treatment of worms for dogs. It is an antispasmodic, stimulates circulation, good for arthritis, dysplasia, sprains and strains, and works well with ginger to treat motion sickness. Because one of the key constituents of peppermint is menthol, this oil should be kept away from your pets' eyes and sensitive skin areas. It can be used topically or orally.

Rosemary is high in fiber, rich in vitamins, anti-oxidant, anti-inflammatory, anti-allergic, anti fungal, anti-septic, disease preventing and health promoting properties.

Sea Salt, in small amounts, is considered safe for dogs. It provides sodium, which is necessary for life. It helps with muscle contraction and expansion, nerve stimulation, the proper functioning of the adrenals, chloride which helps produce acids necessary to digest protein and enzymes for carbohydrate digestion necessary for proper brain functioning and growth, and finally, magnesium which is important for producing enzymes, nerve transmission, bone formation, forming tooth enamel, and resistance to heart disease.

Thyme contains Vitamin K, iron, manganese, calcium, fiber and tryptophan, phytochemicals and anti-oxidants. It has antiseptic, anti-spasmodic, anti-bacterial properties, and is thought to have anti-cancer properties. It's good for the skin, respiratory system, good brain function and gastrointestinal health.

Turmeric has a peppery, warm and bitter flavor and a mild fragrance slightly reminiscent of orange and ginger. It is best known as one of the ingredients used to make curry but it also gives mustard its bright yellow color. Curcumin, the principle active component in turmeric, is a potent anti-inflammatory and antibacterial agent that shows promise in the prevention and treatment of cancer among other conditions. It is generally found to be safe for dogs and cats with veterinarians frequently recommending the addition of turmeric (up to a quarter of a teaspoon per day for every 10 pounds of weight) to a dog or cat's diet if they have been

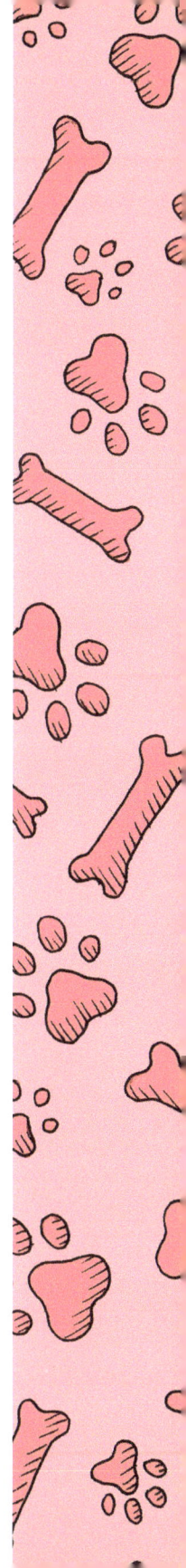

diagnosed with cancer. Turmeric can also be good for reducing arthritis inflammation and pain in pets. You can use powder, crushed or fresh root.

If feeding puppies, pregnant or lactating dogs check with your own Veterinarian before using, as not all herbs and spices are safe.

Herbs and Spices that are not Safe for Dogs

- Cocoa
- Comfrey
- Mace
- Ma Haung (Ephedra)
- Nutmeg
- Paprika
- Pennyroyal
- Pepper
- Table Salt
- Tea Tree Oil
- Wormwood

Canine First Aid and Safety

We can tell you from experience that when you have a medical pet emergency, you need to be already prepared with both the important supplies to take care of your dog as well as the training to do so in the best way possible. So be sure and take the time to make the preparations suggested in this section of our book.

The following information is cross-checked and referenced from a number of sources including:

- The American Veterinary Medical Foundation at http://www.avmf.org
- The American Humane Society at http://www.humanesociety.org/animals/resources/tips/pet_first_aid_kit.html
- The American Red Cross at http://www.redcross.org/prepare/location/home-family/pets/safe-healthy.

From these sources, we have summarized what we think are the key points of information on preparing for pet emergencies and we suggest that you visit the associations we are citing in your local area for further tips, classes, and assistance.

Pet Emergency Basics

To prepare ahead in case of emergency some of the basics you need to keep your pet safe are as follows:

1. Keep phone numbers for your vet, emergency hospital, have a copy (preferably in a water-proof bag) on hand in the car, home and the telephone numbers on the refrigerator door. Give day care a copy as well. And always give pet sitters this information.
2. Have on hand to take to the hospital in case of emergency your pet's medical records, including medications and vaccination history.
3. Veterinarian: Have a regular veterinarian, have the phone number and address (map included is best) of an emergency veterinary clinic with after-hours and weekend care.
4. Animal Poison Control Center: 888-4ANI-HELP (888-426-4435) (there may be a fee for this call).

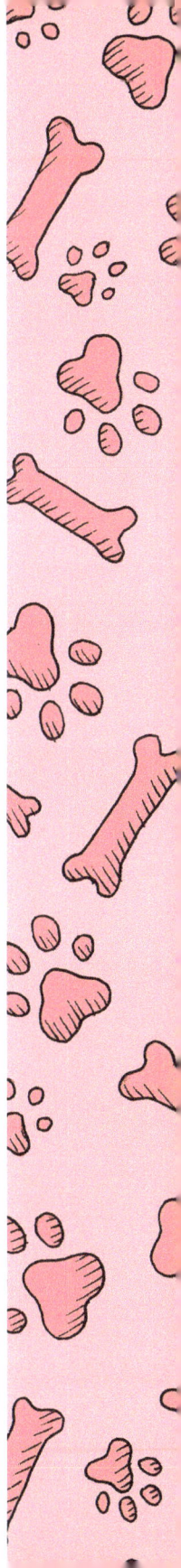

5. Assemble a Pet First Aid Kit and be sure all adult members of the family know where it is at all times. (Keep out of reach of children if your first aid kit includes medications). Also tell your pet sitter where you keep the pet first aid kit. It may include these items:

- A pet first aid book
- Gauze for wrapping wounds or muzzling an injured dog
- Nonstick bandages (that stretches and sticks to itself but not to dog's fur. They are available at pet stores and also from pet-supply catalogs.), towels to control bleeding and protect wounds.
- Adhesive tape for bandages. Do NOT use human adhesive bandages (eg, Band-Aids) on dogs to secure the gauze wrap or bandage.
- Scissors (with blunt ends)
- Milk of magnesia
- Activated charcoal to absorb poison. Always contact your veterinarian or local poison control center before inducing vomiting or treating an animal for poison.
- Hydrogen peroxide (3%)
- Ice pack
- Digital Thermometer. You will need a "fever" thermometer because the temperature scale of regular thermometers doesn't go high enough for pets. To check your pet's temperature, do not insert a thermometer in your pet's mouth- the temperature must be taken rectally.
- Petroleum jelly (to lubricate the thermometer)
- A plastic eye dropper (or large syringe without needle) to give oral treatments or flush wounds
- Tweezers
- Ear cleaning solution for dogs
- Muzzle (in an emergency a rope, necktie, soft cloth, nylon stocking, small towel may be used) to cover your pet's head. If your pet is vomiting, do not muzzle it!
- Leash - To transport your pet (if your pet is capable of walking without further injury)

- Stretcher (in an emergency a door, board, blanket or floor mat may be used) to stabilize the injured animal and prevent further injury during transport
- A few days' supply of any medications (both topical and oral) that your specific dog may need during an emergency away from the home (ask your vet if you have any questions about your dog's specific medication needs). Be sure and check the expiration dates of any medications or supplies in your kit.

Always remember that any first aid administered to your pet should be followed by immediate veterinary care. While first aid care is not a substitute for veterinary care, it may save your pet's life until it receives veterinary treatment.

Pet owners are advised to have a Home Emergency Sticker on their entry window. The sticker informs fire fighters that you have animals (and you can add your children) in your home in case of a fire or other emergency. The sticker alerts the rescue team to "Please Rescue Our Pet In Case of Emergency". These may be obtained from *Maggie's Kitchen Tails: Dog Treat Recipes and Puppy Tales to Love* Gift Store's web site: http://www.MaggieTails.com. A good source for buying other survival emergency dog products including emergency survival dog food and first aid kits is Amazon for a good value. Be sure to watch Maggie's web store for future supplies.

* If you prefer to purchase a ready-made kit, good choices include:

Medi+ Pet Deluxe First Aid Kit - http://www.naturespet.com/firstaidkit.html

The Hiker First Aid Kit for Canines - http://www.ruffwear.com/products/firstaid

If someone is taking care of your pet while you're away: show them where you keep the first aid kit and vet records, your vet and emergency animal hospital info, how to contact you, and the name and phone number of a friend or relative in case you are unavailable. In addition, let your vet know in advance who you have authorized to take your pet to the vet in your absence, and that you will pay for any emergency visit.

Preparing For the Safety of Your Dog During a Disaster

In the event of a disaster, the first thing you want to do to keep your dog safe is bring her inside the house and be sure your dog is wearing a collar with an up-to-date identification tag.

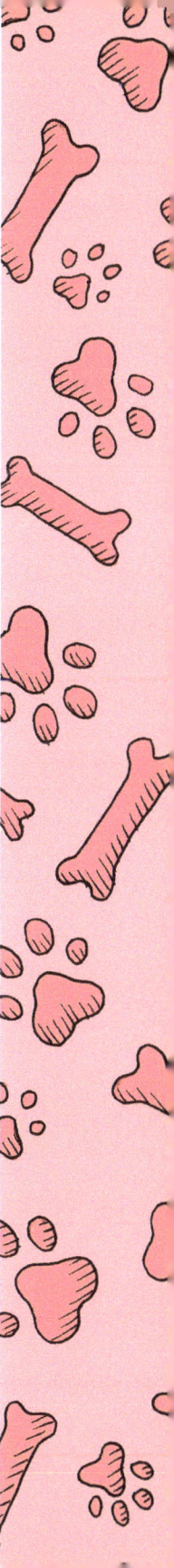

The following tips and more on how to prepare for the safety of your dog during a disaster are made available by the American Red Cross as a printable copy at http://www.redcross.org/images/MEDIA_CustomProductCatalog/m3640126_PetSafety.pdf. We highly advise that you print and follow these preparations before disaster hits. Here is a summary of a few tips to get you started in your preparation for responding to a disaster in a moment's notice: (also a free app is available on line from the American Red Cross for emergency first aid procedures)

1. Assemble and keep on hand an emergency supply kit for your dog, include a first aid kit, leases, a sturdy pet carrier, food, drinking water, bowls, medications, and copies of medical records.

2. Also have with your emergency kit, current photos of you and your dog with contact information (phone numbers of vet, relatives or friends who might keep your dog, emergency clinic, animal boarding facilities, etc.).

3. Include records of your dog's current vaccinations as they may be required for emergency boarding.

4. Include with emergency kit a dog bed or bedding and toys.

Remember that while Red Cross Shelters accept dogs that are service animals, they usually do not accept dogs in general and you may have to find a separate place for your dog to stay from the rest of the family. For this reason, you may wish to locate and have the numbers and addresses of hotels or motels in your area that are dog friendly or that take dogs in case of disaster emergency.

American Red Cross Dog First Aid Classes on Pet Disaster and Safety

The American Red Cross has developed Dog First Aid with comprehensive guides to help keep your dog healthy and safe. Learn how to respond to canine health emergencies and to provide basic first aid for your dog. Practice and preparation will help you be calm and effective in an emergency, protecting you and your dog from further injury or suffering. Sign up for Dog First Aid, Cat First Aid, or Cat and Dog First Aid. Course length is 2 1/2 – 3 1/2 hours depending on course option selected.

The Pet First Aid course includes:

    Understanding basic pet owner responsibilities

    Administering medicine

    Managing breathing and cardiac emergencies

    Managing urgent care situation

    Treating wounds

    Treating electrical shock

    Caring for eye, foot and ear injuries

    Preparing for disasters

For more information on American Red Cross Pet First Aid Classes and to find a class in your area go to http://www.redcross.org/take-a-class/program-highlights/cpr-first-aid/wilderness-sports-pets/.

CANINE HEALTH CARE ASSISTANCE

Sometimes unexpected circumstances happen and our pets need medical care that may be beyond our ability to afford. For this reason, we advise looking into Pet Health Insurance. There are a number of agencies that are recommended including Pet Plan (see http://www.gopetplan.com) recommended by The Humane Society.

The Humane Society also has an extensive list of national organizations (see www.humanesociety.org/animals/resources/tips/trouble_affording_pet.html?credit=web_id100 104631) that provide financial assistance for pet medical needs including prescription medication, cancer, heart disease, and senior dogs. Examples are: Paws For a Cure and The Pet Fund that gives financial assistance for injured and ill dogs, and helps with finances for surgeries. If you are having trouble with financing medical needs for your dog, be sure and take a look at this extensive list and what is available in your state on the Human Society website at the internet address above.

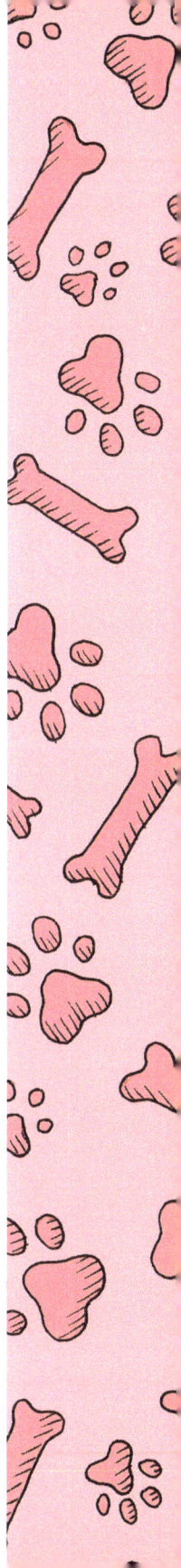

Some General Dog Safety Tips

We have accumulated a list of dog safety tips for car and home from The American Humane Society. Many of these you most likely already follow, but do read over this list because many are life saving tips:

1. Do not let your dog ride in an open flat bed truck or vehicle. Any sudden stop or vehicle movement may toss your dog onto the highway where it can get hit by oncoming traffic. The American Human Society estimates that at least 100,000 dogs die this way each year.
2. Do not leash your dog inside the truck bed as they may be tossed while riding and strangled.
3. If your dog must ride in the back of a truck, put the dog inside a crate that will give it some protection and tie the crate securely to the walls of the truck bed.
4. Be sure your dog's head and paws are inside the car.
5. Check your dog's collar every week for correct neck size, particularly while your dog is still growing up (until age 1 year).
6. In your home, place medications, cleaners, chemicals, and laundry supplies on high shelves so your dog can not get into them.
7. Keep the toilet lid closed to prevent drowning or drinking of harmful cleaning chemicals by your dog.
8. Place dangling wires from lamps, VCRs, televisions, stereos, and telephones out of reach of your puppy.
9. Make sure all heating/air vents have covers.
10. Check all those places where your vacuum cleaner doesn't fit, but your puppy does, for dangerous items, like string.
11. Be sure all sewing and craft notions are put away when not being used, especially thread!
12. Be sure and look out for paws, noses, and tails when you shut doors or scoot chairs.

FROM ASPCA
http://www.petmd.com/dog/care/evr_multi_top10_emergency_pet_kit_items

In the event of an emergency they recommend the following tips or supplies to have on hand when shopping for emergency supplies for your family don't forget your pets.

1. WATER-store enough water for one week for each person in your family including your pet
2. Food: Canned food is recommended as it stores longer and the moisture will help with hydration. Don't forget the can opener.
3. Medications: Make arrangements with your Veterinarian for medicines for any chronic conditions so you have an emergency supply on hand.
4. Be sure to keep a record of all medical records and vaccinations. In an emergency if you need to board your pet the clinic may require proof of vaccines being up to date.
5. Keep a list of helpful contacts for your friends, neighbors or boarding facilities you can rely on in an emergency to keep your pet safe in an emergency.
6. Keep copies of proof of ownership for your pet in a tight waterproof container to protect it from damage. You may need proof of ownership should you be separated from your pet or need to board them. Keep items such as photographs and copies of your identity in case you are forced to go to a shelter in an emergency.
7. Keep a couple of leashes and/or pet carriers on hand both in the house and automobiles. In an emergency, power lines and debris may be down making it difficult to get around one their own. Your leashes will enable you to assist them also keeping them from drinking contaminated ground water and the crates will be a safe haven for them when frightened.
8. Be sure to have Identification Tags on hand to fit them with quickly so that you can be reunited with them in the event you become separated Please be sure to keep the records current.
9. First Aid kit is critical to treat any injuries such as cuban type bandages, anti-biotic ointment, surgical scissors, and milk of magnesia to absorb poison should accidental ingestion occur.

Last but so important are the comforts from home: pet bed, blankets, pillows, toys towels and a bone or chew toy. These items can assist you with keeping your canine calm in an emergency.

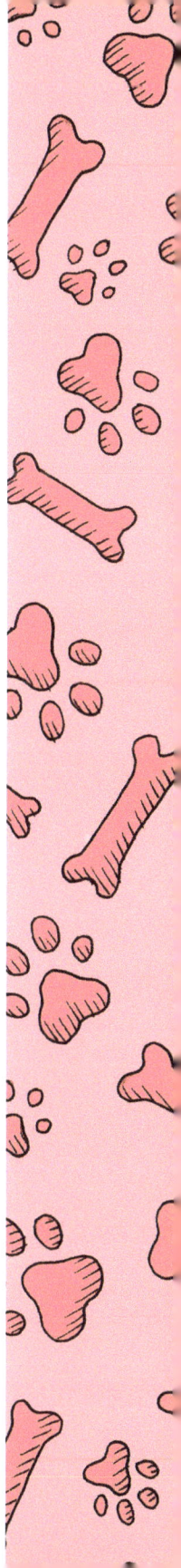

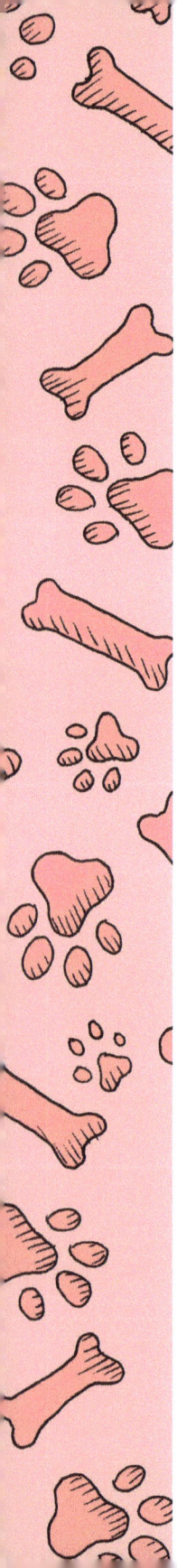

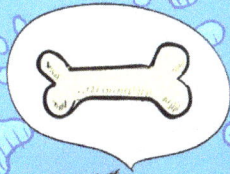

the grey gull

POOL · SPA · SAUNA

CHASE ENTERPRISES PUBLISHING

Naturally 4 Paws

Your Total Health Store for Pets

🐾 Natural Supplies   🐾 Grooming   🐾 Training
🐾 Massage Therapy   🐾 Self-Serve Bathing

All Natural Pet Supplies

RALPH'S Red Apple MARKET

POULSBO Red Apple MARKET

SPONSORS

GREY GULL RESORT
CHASE ENTERPRISES PUBLISHING
NATURALLY 4 PAWS
RALPH'S RED APPLE

The Grey Gull Ocean Beach Resort

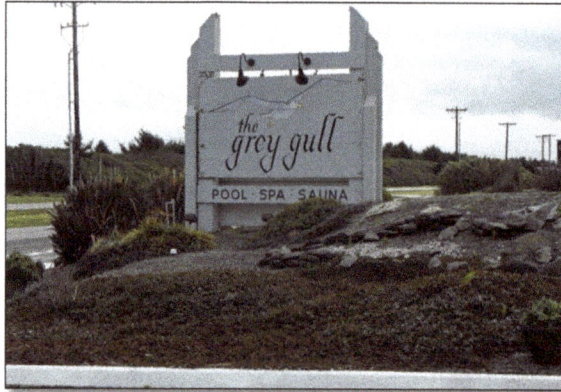

Located in the heart of Washington's finest resort community, Ocean Shores is just a short, scenic drive from Seattle or Portland. The Grey Gull's 37 unique and charming, independently-owned condominiums feature gas fireplaces, fully equipped kitchens in most units, and ocean or pool views. Whether your visit is brief, long-term, or you are looking to purchase, we have the perfect accommodations to suit your needs.

Dog Friendly Lodging

Welcome, Fido! What is a trip to the beach without your favorite pooch? Bring your best friend, and we will provide doggie bed bags and treats upon check in. View our Dog Friendly units and kindly review our Pet Owner's Agreement for rules.

Privately Owned Condominiums

Our condo units are not the typical hotel room. Each has its owners' personal touch expressed by their units' particular style and décor. With west-facing windows, balconies, and porches, all of our guests can enjoy a breathtaking view of a sunset or relax while keeping an eye on the kids playing in the pool. Our condos have clean burning gas fireplaces, free WIFI internet access, cable television, and DVD players. The full kitchens feature the conveniences of home with all major appliances, cookware and tableware provided. Studio Suites are equipped with kitchenettes and include a two-burner stove top, small refrigerator, and microwave. Come delight in the comfort and out-of-the-ordinary experience of The Grey Gull.

Ocean Shores is a wonderful combination of small town life in a beautiful setting that over 3 million people come to visit every year. Beautiful, secluded old growth woodlands, excellent dining with a wide assortment of cuisines, restful public parks, 18 hole public golf course, and miles of fresh water lakes & canals for fishing and water sports. We also have lots of shops and specialty stores. Regular events and festivals bring plenty of exciting and interesting people to Ocean Shores.

The Pacific Ocean to the west, Grays Harbor to the east, and canals and lakes in between add to the maritime and recreational draw for tourists, fishermen, boaters and residents. Abundant wildlife in Ocean Shores making bird-watching, whale watching, and photo ops with the neighborhood deer families some of our best attractions.

The Grey Gull opened in 1969 and is one of the longest operating hotels in Ocean Shores. Designed by world renowned architect Ralph Anderson, The Grey Gull was uniquely built to resemble the soaring wings of the seagull. Originally envisioned as a beach lodge, the hotel featured large log columns, open beamed ceilings, and a brick fireplace in the great room. These features can still be seen today.

http://www.thegreygull.com/

My name is Clayton Bye. I'm a writer, editor and publisher. The author of 11 books, just as many ghostwrites, a varied collection of short stories, poems, articles and reviews, I've also published 4 books under the imprint Chase Enterprises Publishing. These books, published for others, include 3 award winning anthologies and a stunning memoir about what it's like to live with and die from anorexia.

I also offer a wide range of writing related services, including small business management for writers.

Visit his e-store at http://shop.claytonbye.com or his website at www.claytonbye.com

Chase Enterprises Publishing
Box 2922,
Kenora, Ontario, Canada
P9N 4C8
1 (807) 466-7642
ccbye@shaw.ca

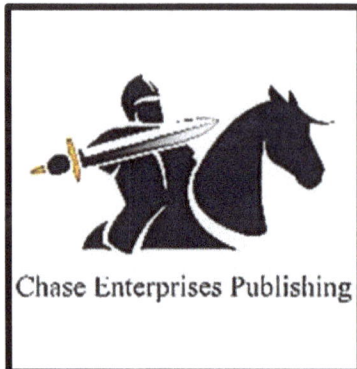

My story … I've been publishing for 20+ years. It's been a lot of work but great fun. As most writers, I was never able to support myself writing full time. It wasn't until I became unable to work at my regular job due to severe Rheumatoid Arthritis throughout my joints and the subsequent arrival of uncontrollable Bi-Polar Depression that I was afforded an amazing opportunity. Once doctors managed to bring me back to a modicum of health, I found that if I positioned myself on a couch with my legs stretched out and pillows at my back I didn't hurt. So, out came my laptop and I began to write. I had to take many breaks, but I kept at it eight hours per day, every day. Years passed and many books were published, but I was still unable to supplement my pension to any great degree. Then, in November of 2014, I stumbled into a full-time ghostwriting job. Again, it did not replace my pension, but it was a terrific step up. Now, in May 2015, I'm taking a unique copywriting course and have begun to break into the lucrative world of the copywriter.

I tell you these things because I'm a firm believer in the idea that we can achieve our dreams if only we will act and persevere. It may have taken me 20 years to become a full-time writer (I could survive on my writing wages if it weren't for horrendous medical costs), but I made it. Now there is nowhere to go but up.

You should also understand that the 20 year journey I made truly was fun; it was worth all the effort and the some-times meager returns. I love the pastimes of writing, editing, doing book formatting and layout, cover designs and the final rush of sending books to my printer.

Yes, I'm a self-publisher. I was doing this before anyone ever heard of print-on demand (POD), back when you had to do a run of at least a thousand books in order to get your book costs down to an affordable rate. Traditional publishing was something I never considered. Maybe I could have made my fortune if I did. But I had all these skills I wanted to use—so away I went.

During all these years of writing, I married and raised three wonderful children, who are all in university at this time. Living in the heart of Sunset Country, on beautiful Lake of the Woods in Kenora, Ontario, Canada, I also carved out a wonderful place amidst the rich Masonic community that exists here. I believe I am respected in the business community, but I've never worried much about it. I've worked hard as a newspaper man, a Life insurance agent and as a sales representative for Frito-Lay Canada. All great jobs. But the world-wide business community I work within as a writer is the most rich and rewarding of them all. I've met and befriended people all over the world and, now, with the advent of Skype it's like these people have come right into the in-home office where I spend my days.

One of the greatest rewards of them all, however, was the trip I took this spring to meet, in person, my dear friend Mamie Adkins. She and her husband, Doug, are two of the most genuine and lovable people I know, and they opened their home and their hearts to me. Now, as they work so hard on their special project *Maggie's Kitchen Tails*, I have the pleasure of sponsoring their effort to help rescue dogs in need of loving homes. I hope you enjoy this cookbook and the stories it contains.

Clayton Clifford Bye, May 30th, 2015

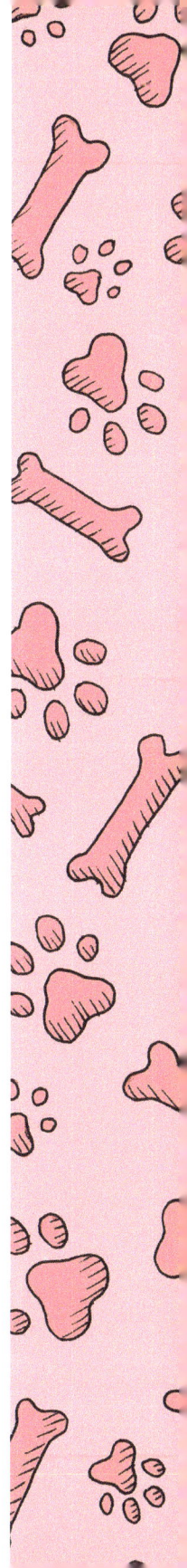

Naturally 4 Paws

Long ago in a land far, far away we use to feed our beloved Shetland Sheepdog, Goephyr, with a national brand of dog food (whose name has been withheld to protect the not-so-innocent) sold at local grocery stores. At the time we didn't know any better. When Goephyr developed Cushing's Disease we immediately started researching the pet food industry and what we learned about the ingredients in that bag shocked us!

Goephyr's food was filled with artificial and unhealthy ingredients, cooked at a temperature that destroys most of the nutritional benefits, and likely was a major contributing factor to his disease. We were aghast, ashamed and vowed that none of our future friends would be subjected to such low quality food.

Naturally 4 Paws is locally owned and operated by two Seabeck residents who got tired of long road trips to find good quality products for their three new family members (Rascal, Rusty and Rowdy). So we opened our own store in Silverdale to provide our local community with the best the pet industry has to offer.

Although we appreciate the efforts of the mega-national chain stores and the boom they've helped to create in the pet industry, they don't focus on all-natural, organic or holistic products, nor do they have the education and knowledge base required in the world of animal nutrition. So we created a "Pet Health Food Store" and vowed to provide the best customer service environment possible.

We also decided to focus on community education and outreach. How many other loving pet owners (like we once were) are out there feeding their best friends food that isn't healthy for them? Animals that are fed a natural, healthy diet live longer and happier lives; have fewer behavioral problems, and visit the vet's office much less frequently (don't get us wrong, we love vets… it's just that we want our visits to be limited to regular check-ups with a clean bill of health and not for emergency visits or long-term terminal illnesses).

Although holistic and organic foods do cost more than those "big store" brands, the savings are realized through stronger, healthier and happier companions, which in turn means less expensive vet visits. We ran across a startling statistic that states that the average dog owner will spend over $15,000 during the course of their pet's life. Of that total, over $11,000 typically goes to vets for treatments of diseases, allergies and terminal illnesses. We surmise that spending a little more on a healthy diet will actually save money in the long run… and making our fur-kids healthier and happier at the same time. And isn't that the goal of all animal lovers?

Our philosophy is that animals aren't just pets, they are part of our families and our focus is on their health and happiness.

Our mission is to provide a wide variety of healthy food and treats, unique and high quality accessories, while bringing back good old fashioned customer service. We strive to carry American goods whenever possible and thoroughly investigate each food product manufacturer. Our goal is to explain and promote the benefits of feeding holistic diets. We encourage pet guardians to be responsible and accountable and are eager to assist in strengthening the human & animal bond.

We hope you will come in and visit our store. At Naturally 4 Paws, animals are not just pets, they are part of our family and our focus is on enriching that bond between you and your animals.

Naturally 4 Paws
9337 Silverdale Way NW
(Silverdale Village)
Silverdale, WA 98383

RED APPLE MARKET

Ralph's and Poulsbo Red Apple Market have both been in existence for well over 60 years. Starting out as Shop Rite Stores they both changed to the Red Apple format in the 1990's. Today, as in the past, they are committed to serving the community and delivering to "BEST" quality perishables around including meat, produce, deli and bakery departments. Even though it's hard, work we at Red Apple still like to have a fun working environment. When we used to have a night stocking crew we would set up a make shift bowling alley down the aisle to play on our breaks. There were times that in order to wake Casey up in the morning we would throw a firecracker under his chair! Good thing he has a sense of humor!

Sponsors

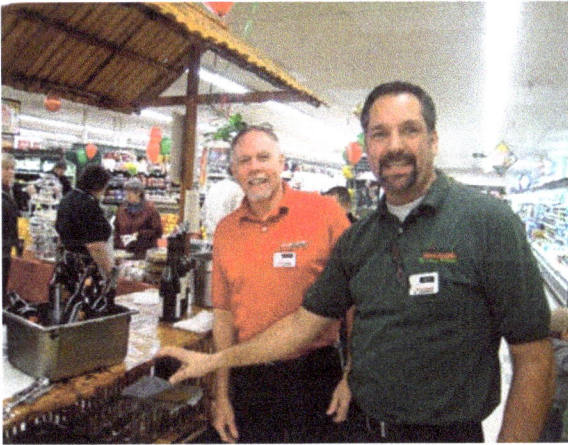

Glyn and Jeff

Today's owners Jeff Uberuaga and Glyn Correll still take pride in creating a fun and pleasant atmosphere to work in while providing excellent customer service seven (7) days a week. Jeff and Glyn invite everyone to stop in and see what the Red Apple has to offer. While at Ralph's stop and say hello to John in the Produce, Casey in the Meat, Louann in the Deli and Jeff in the Bakery department. In Poulsbo see Rodger in the Meat, Mike in Produce and Emma in the Deli & Bakery department.

A special thanks to long time employee and friend Glen Osterhaus for these fun facts!

Locally Owned & Operated

Red Apple MARKETS

Ralph's Red Apple
6724 Kitsap Way
Bremerton
360-377-5708

Poulsbo Red Apple
2044 Viking Ave NW
Poulsbo
360-779-4422

Go BlueJackets!

193

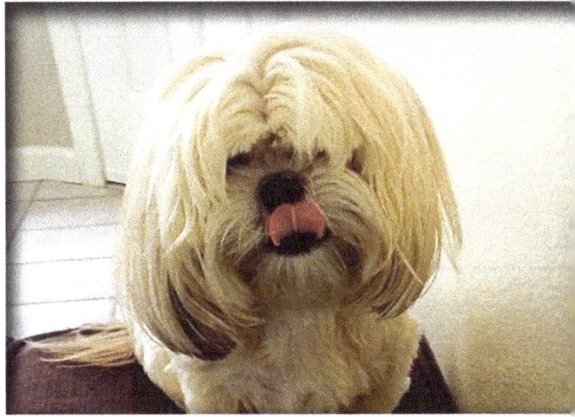

Zakariya Sherman,
Branch Manager Kitsap Regional Library

ABOUT THE AUTHORS

Rosemary "Mamie" Adkins- Douglas Adkins
and Maggie Anne Adkins, Rescued and Loved

Martha char Love and Grand Puppy
Momo always loved

Rosemary "Mamie" Adkins

Rosemary "Mamie" Adkins, preferring to be addressed as Mamie, was born and raised in Houston, Texas with her parents and two brothers, later moving to Las Vegas, Nevada and graduating from Bishop Gorman High School. Mamie had been raised in a family of five growing up with two wonderful brothers. But her life was surrounded with a great deal of sadness stemming from abuse. She learned at an early age of four to stand alone being brave, never giving up in spite of the horrid torment from both mental and physical abuse. Mamie says that in spite of the abuse, she learned to appreciate the love now present in her life—love that made her even more determined to reach out to the abused, both human and dogs. In many ways her difficult life has given her the ability to see forward into the future, planning her journeys rather than just allowing fate to take her there. Mamie vowed to one day make a difference in the life of others and set her plans for when she would be finally on her own. After graduation she drifted until she found her way in life and settled in Bremerton, Washington in 1985. Here she found her peace on earth by the sea and married, raising a beautiful daughter whom she is very proud of.

Except for a few years in a community college, most of what she learned in life for education was from the school of hard knocks but the one dream that remained a constant was her desire to write, becoming an author.

In 2011, she and her husband traveled to Ireland, realizing another dream. This is where her first book was completed and titled *Extraordinary Dreams of an Ireland Traveler*. In this book she shares her journey through the country with her husband, taking you along as her friends and sharing the high points of places to visit.

Writing this book gave Mamie the courage to complete the book she had struggled with for over sixteen years. It was published in 2012 and was a memoir in which Mamie had to deal with the demons in her life and relive the abuse she suffered in life from age four to fifty-five. One huge benefit from the completion of this book was that it set her free. Titled *Reflections of*

About The Authors

The latest book release is no different except her husband, Douglas, is a co-author of *Maggie's Kitchen Tails: Dog Treat Recipes and Puppy Tales to Love*. This book will launch on Halloween—October 31, 2015 in honor of their family rescue dog, Maggie, who will turn two years of age on that date. Mamie and Doug spent time volunteering at the Kitsap Humane Society for their puppy fix, after losing their beloved dog, Sandy, of eleven years who died from Cancer complications. They did not expect to find another dog let alone an abused puppy at the age of eight weeks. But love took them into another direction of writing this new book which is a short story book combined with healthy dog treat recipes. Mamie and Doug wanted to help abused animals with the profits from the sale of their book with hopes these abused and abandoned dogs would find new homes and loving families. Mamie and Doug were lucky again in life to have a friend who is a successful author and compassionate about dogs. They were happy that she, Martha Char Love, agreed to join them in this journey to help so many dogs in despair.

Mamie has no hobbies to speak of but enjoys quilting and beach walking—looking for glass floats and special treasures. Mamie says she lives to write every day of her life and feels incomplete if she does not find something to write about. "Writing gives me the gladness in my heart."

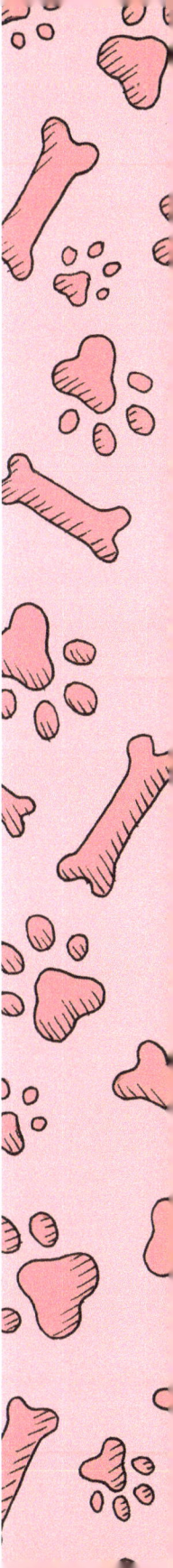

Douglas Adkins

Douglas Adkins was born and raised in Great Falls, Montana with his parents and five siblings. The love and nurturing he learned at home gave him the insight to become the man he is today, respecting the vows of marriage and raising a wonderful daughter.

Doug, after graduation from high school, went on to college for a few years before joining the United States Navy where he spent ten years attached to the submarine service. Time in the Navy sent him in many directions, including Hawaii, where he spent five years at Pearl Harbor.

Following the ten years in the Navy, he secured employment at the Puget Sound Naval Shipyard where he worked in the engineering department and overseeing the ships' maintenance and construction. Doug loved his work and writing was no stranger to him as he wrote many testing programs for the maintenance of the ships worked.

Doug spent several years as a bachelor but in 1988 he married Rosemary "Mamie" and together they raised their daughter, Kecia, in Bremerton, Washington. He was an active parent in the life of his daughter and the family was as close as what he had known growing up.

His greatest love for living is to be near the mountains, but he shares his wife's love of the sea, feeling as though they live in the perfect place being close to both the mountains and the sea.

Retiring after 30 years at the shipyard his first great vacation was a dream of a lifetime—traveling to Ireland. He was retired all of two weeks when his wife decided to import Irish woollen accessories, so back to work he went. And although he loved Ireland, he sure tried to explain what retirement was supposed to look like! Trade shows around the country, dealing with customs and selling to the retail stores were not his idea of retirement, yet he found time to assist his wife in completing her book about their Ireland journey! There were many times he had wished he could go back to the shipyard, retiring again but this time the right way!

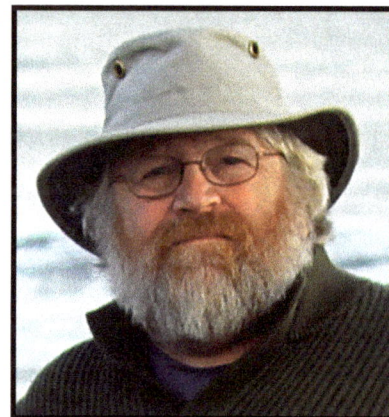

About The Authors

As time moved on, Doug found himself writing schedules, letters, doing promotions and traveling to promote his wife's second book. No, he had not yet retired and was busier than ever and getting less sleep than when he worked fifty hours a week!

In 2013, he and his wife had been volunteering at the Humane Society and KARE when they found a new eight week old puppy that needed a home and they fell in love with her. Of course, he says, they had forgotten what it was like to raise a puppy! Hours and days that turned into months of training, playing and living the schedule that catered to his dog was now his life.

In the course of raising their new puppy, Maggie, Doug became an author. He and his wife wanted to write a book about the journeys they took raising their new puppy and the recipes that they had to learn for a healthy dog since Maggie had been so ill when first adopted.

Together they began writing *Maggie's Kitchen Tails*. And when they felt their dear friend, who is also compassionate about dogs, would add both expertise and enjoyment, they asked Martha Char Love to join them. Now they all spend their time researching and writing the book called, *Maggie's Kitchen Tails: Dog Treat Recipes and Puppy Tales to Love.*

Doug has no hobbies and says/ he would not know where there could be time for anything else but loving his dog, taking her for walks and knowing she will never be harmed again.

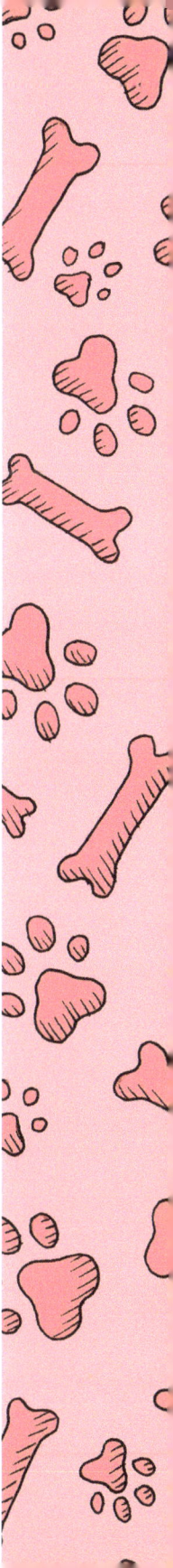

Martha Char Love

Martha Char Love is originally from Atlanta, Georgia, where she was raised and completed her Master's Degree at the University of Georgia in School Psychology. Yes, she's a true Georgia Peach! As an adult, she worked as a professional educator for over 10 years in schools in both Mississippi and Florida, before moving to Santa Rosa, California.

There in northern California, she and her beloved husband, Michael (Zardoa) Love, and their two children lived for over 25 years. Martha preferred being a stay-at-home parent and worked at home as a clothing dye artist while raising her children and selling her art at craft fairs, in which the entire family could participate. Martha says that being a mom was the light of her life and while she had to change her profession and life style to have the time to be home with her children, she would in a heartbeat do it the same way all over again.

When her children where young adults, she decided it was time to return to school and update her credentials in psychology. She worked her way through school once again by taking extra computer classes and becoming a computer lab and teaching assistant for seven years in a large local community college. She says that this was one of her favorite jobs because, at that time in the early 2000's, there were many people in need of learning computer skills to enter the 21st century job market and she enjoyed the opportunity of tutoring them this important life skill. While working in the computer lab, Martha went on to complete a second Master's Degree in Depth Psychology and also a post Master's Degree in Art Therapy. It was at this time that she also had the opportunity to teach undergraduate classes in psychology (something she had loved doing earlier in her professional career) and begin her research and writing in psychology.

Martha is now retired and lives in Oahu, Hawaii, with her husband. Very soon into her retirement years, she discovered that she loves to write about a variety of subjects! Since her retirement in 2008, she has published a number of books including *What's Behind Your Belly Button? A Psychological Perspective of the Intelligence of Human Nature and Gut Instinct,* which she co-authored with her colleague of 40 years, Robert W. Sterling. This groundbreaking book is a narrative of the maturation of sciences of psychology and neurology that explores gut feeling intelligence and is based on their research and career experiences as guidance counselors, educators, and school psychologists. They are presently working on a companion book to be released in 2016 titled *Ageing With Instincts.*

In 2014, Martha also published a cookbook titled *Mom's Island Bakens: Over 50 Altered Recipes for a Happy Gut and Healthy Heart,* which she wrote to help people improve their lifestyle choices for healthy eating and it shares her original recipes for a happy gut and a healthy heart. And she has also contributed as a co-author to many of the 34 books written and published with her husband under the pen name The Silver Elves, both fiction and non-fiction, on magic and enchantment. Their new release in May 2015 is *Faerie Unfolding: The Cosmic Expression of the Divine Magic.* All of Martha's books are available on Amazon.com.

Martha became seriously interested in cooking dog food treats for the dogs in her life in 2013 when her Shih Tzu grand dog, Momo, was suspected of having severe food allergies. Sure enough, nutritional tests indicated that Momo is highly allergic to many common ingredients in commercial dog food and dog treats. Once the family began researching the ingredients in Momo's commercially bought food and treats, it was surprising how many dog food brands use the ingredients Momo is allergic to in their products. With the difficulty in finding treats that Momo could eat and not get sick, Martha decided to research healthy diets and nutrition for dogs and create some home cooked treats herself that would fit Momo's particular dietary needs. While baking treats for Momo, Martha also enjoyed cooking for some of her dog friends in her apartment building and further learned the value of doggie home cooking! She says that in many ways, cooking for the dogs in her life feels like she has returned to the nurturing activities of motherhood that she loved so much when her own children were young.

She has always loved dogs and shares with you tales about her adventures with Momo and the many other dogs that have been in her life. Martha wholeheartedly joins Mamie and Doug in their overall goal to help fund animal shelters that save, love, and re-home abused or abandoned dogs.

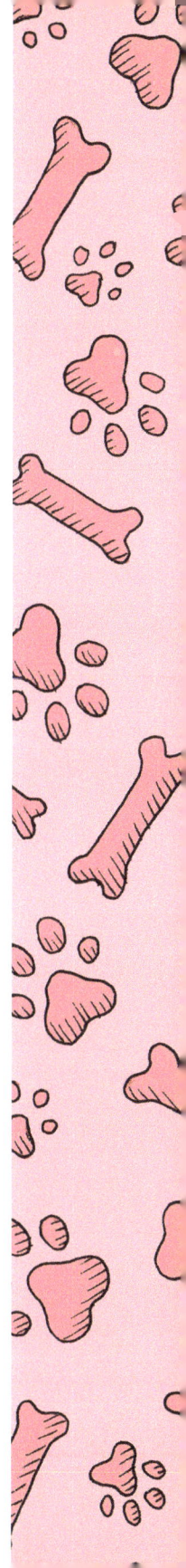

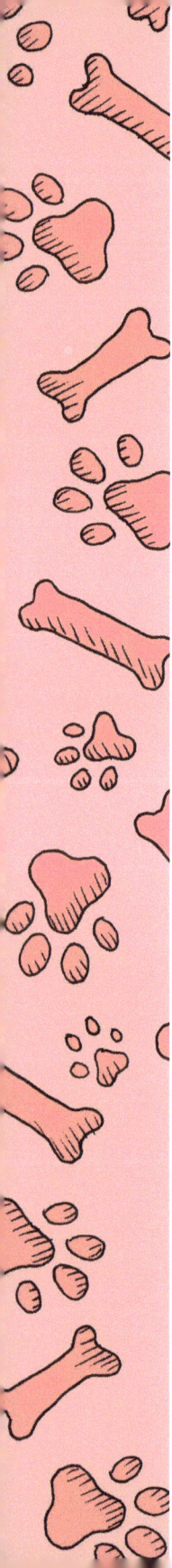

design

BEHIND THE SCENES

BEHIND THE SCENES MAKE OUR BOOK SPECIAL JUST FOR YOU!

If you have never published a book, perhaps you have no idea what it takes to become a reality. You may be thinking that was a dumb statement as writing is what it takes. You would be partially correct but the friends, family and professionals behind each page is more correct.

Writing is the fun part and could take months or years to complete depending on how many re-writes you do. As an author is writing, they make that decision on how they care to illustrate their words so they may elect to use photographs, drawings, clip art or a combination of them all.

This is when a search is on for that perfect Illustrator that understands your subject! They may spend hours or months drawing that perfect piece of art.

But now the time has come for editing which can take almost as long as writing. Their time is spent re-reading every word written looking at each punctuation mark while checking spelling and grammar. Heck, they even need to be sure each photograph is properly placed by reference in the story.

Lastly, comes the Graphic Artist for the layout to be sure each page is tweaked, special effects are where they need to be and general formatting is as perfect as possible.

Please meet our team:

Douglas E. Adkins-Author of Doug's Corner.

Rosemary "Mamie" Adkins, Author.

Martha Char Love, Author.

Clayton Clifford Bye, Editor/Sponsor.

Duncan Fyffe, Graphic Artist

Isabelle Dore, Illustrator.

Maggie Anne Adkins, Rescue and Inspiration Family Dog

Momo Rhodes, Inspiration and Loved Family Dog

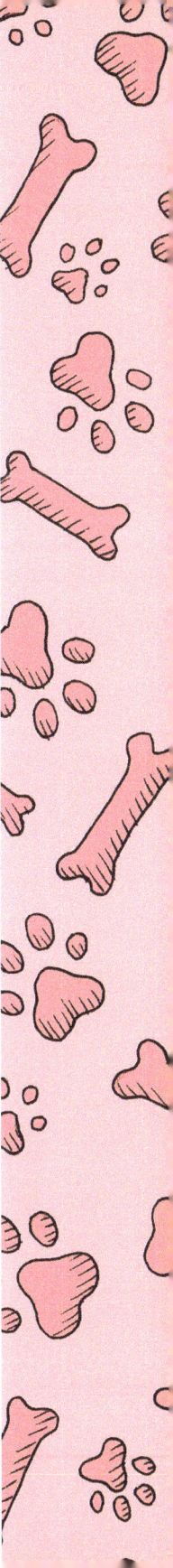

Isabelle Dorr - Artist

Isabelle Dorr is a 14-year old artist who has been drawing ever since she could hold a crayon. Her favorite subjects to draw have always been animals, mainly dogs and fish, or anything else that inspires her. Isabelle recognizes that her talents are a blessing from God, therefore it is important to her to use them to bless others when such opportunities arise. Isabelle enjoys working with a variety of mediums, but her most favorite is colored pencil. Pencil allows her to be very detailed, and gives her the realistic results she enjoys.

Besides art, Isabelle is passionate about fish and has numerous aquariums scattered about her home, including an outdoor goldfish pond. Her mini-zoo also boasts a cuddly crested gecko, two sweet cats, and one high-strung dog. Isabelle, her critters, and her extensive art supplies happily dwell with her mom and dad in Poulsbo, WA.

Below are some samples of her art.

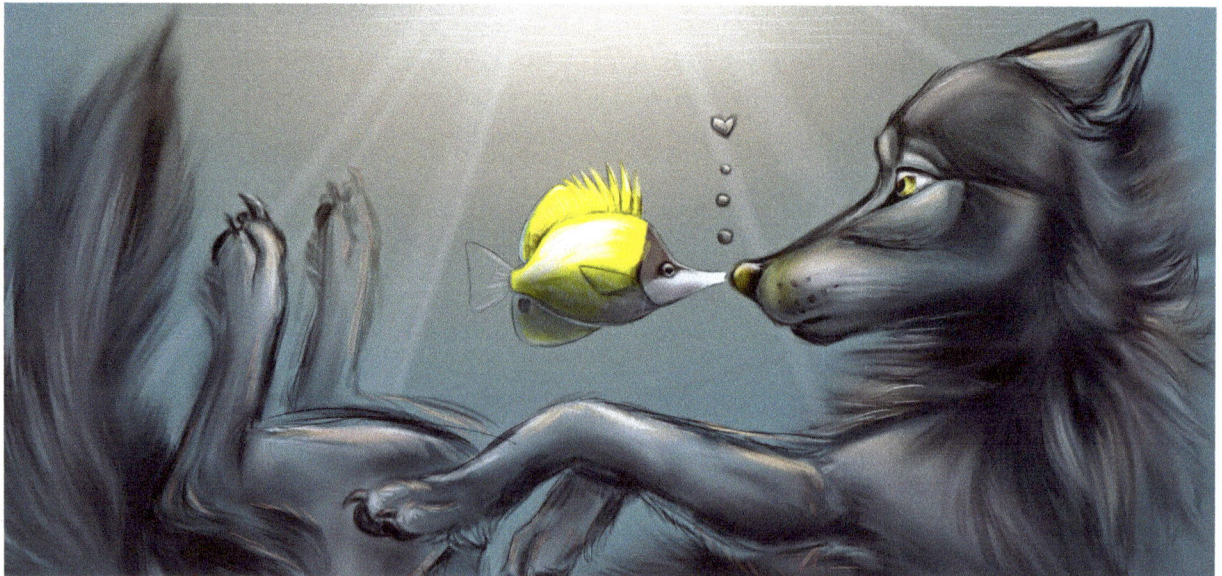

The drawing below, that Isabelle's mother, Michelle, shared on Facebook was an instant success. This young, gifted artist, shared most of her proceeds from sales with the childrens cancer hospital in Seattle, Washington. At a yound age, Isabelle shows both a talented career and a compasionate spirit.

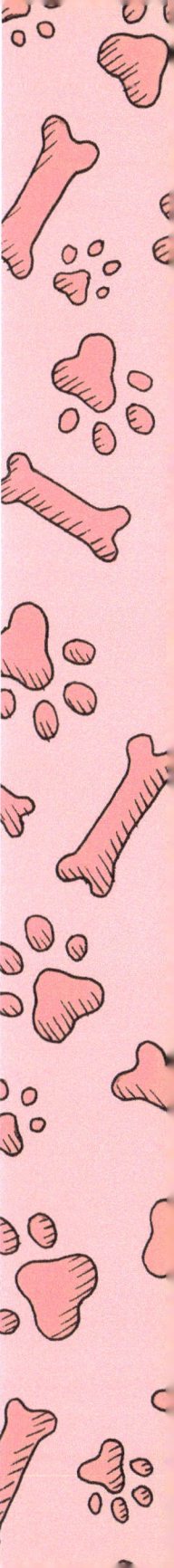

design

DUNCAN FYFFE
Graphic Designer

—— ABOUT & CONTACT ——

Name: Duncan McIntosh Fyffe

Email: silvercyborg@hotmail.com

Interests: Family
Church
Graphics
Music
Outdoors

—— DESIGN SERVICES ——

B r o c h u r e s
Business Cards
Custom Logos
E n v e l o p e s
F l i e r s
Infographics
L e t t e r h e a d
M e n u s
P o s t c a r d s
P o s t e r s
Rack Cards
S i g n s

—— SOFTWARE KNOWLEDGE ——

Adobe :	: Microsoft
Indesign -	- Word
Illustrator -	- Excel
Photoshop -	- Powerpoint
	- Publisher

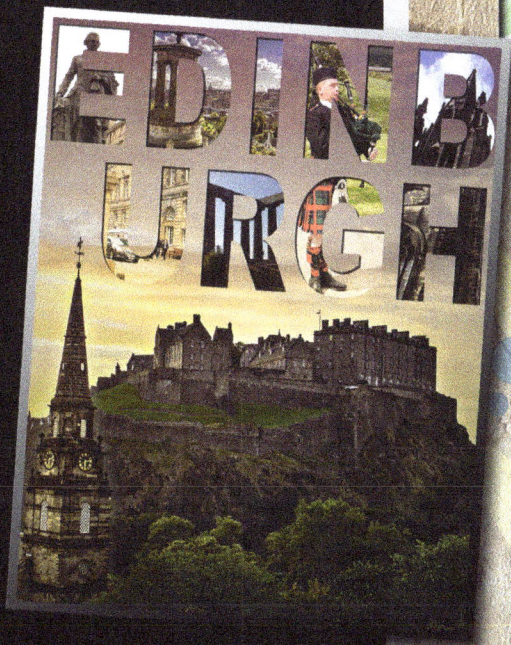

MAGGIE'S FRIENDS

We leave you with a few of Maggie's friends as they are also our friends. Doug, Martha and myself, Mamie know you will enjoy these recipes and find a favorite for your best friend. Maggie has many friends and more than could join us here but wants to thank Momo for being one of her very best friends. The two of them brought to you most of the stories in our book through their inspiration, love and willingness to share their friendship with every dog in the Universe!

Please remember the rescue dogs, abandoned and abused dogs that fill the shelters. and be kind to your own.

Perhaps you will consider baking a few extra treats and sharing them with the dogs that have nothing, maybe even becoming a volunteer taking them for walks or a Foster Parent so they don't have to live out their lives in cages while waiting for some forever home to come their way.

Our dogs are so innocent, give so freely and love unconditionally. They are not your possession or just your pet but a part of your family.

GYPSY HAZEN

A special tribute to a sweet dog who crossed over the Rainbow Bridge just before publishing. We wish to dedicate our book to her and all of our family furry friends we have said goodbye to in the past. Our hearts are saddened but filled with loving memories. Open your hearts and adopt a friend that needs you.

Behind Fence: Buddy the donkey, Mr. Llama
Slide: Maggie, Momo
Middle Row: Merlin Kramer, Hershey & Dextor Doke, Aloha, Jilly Cherry
Front Row: Skippy & Penny Hayes, Kozi Karlsen

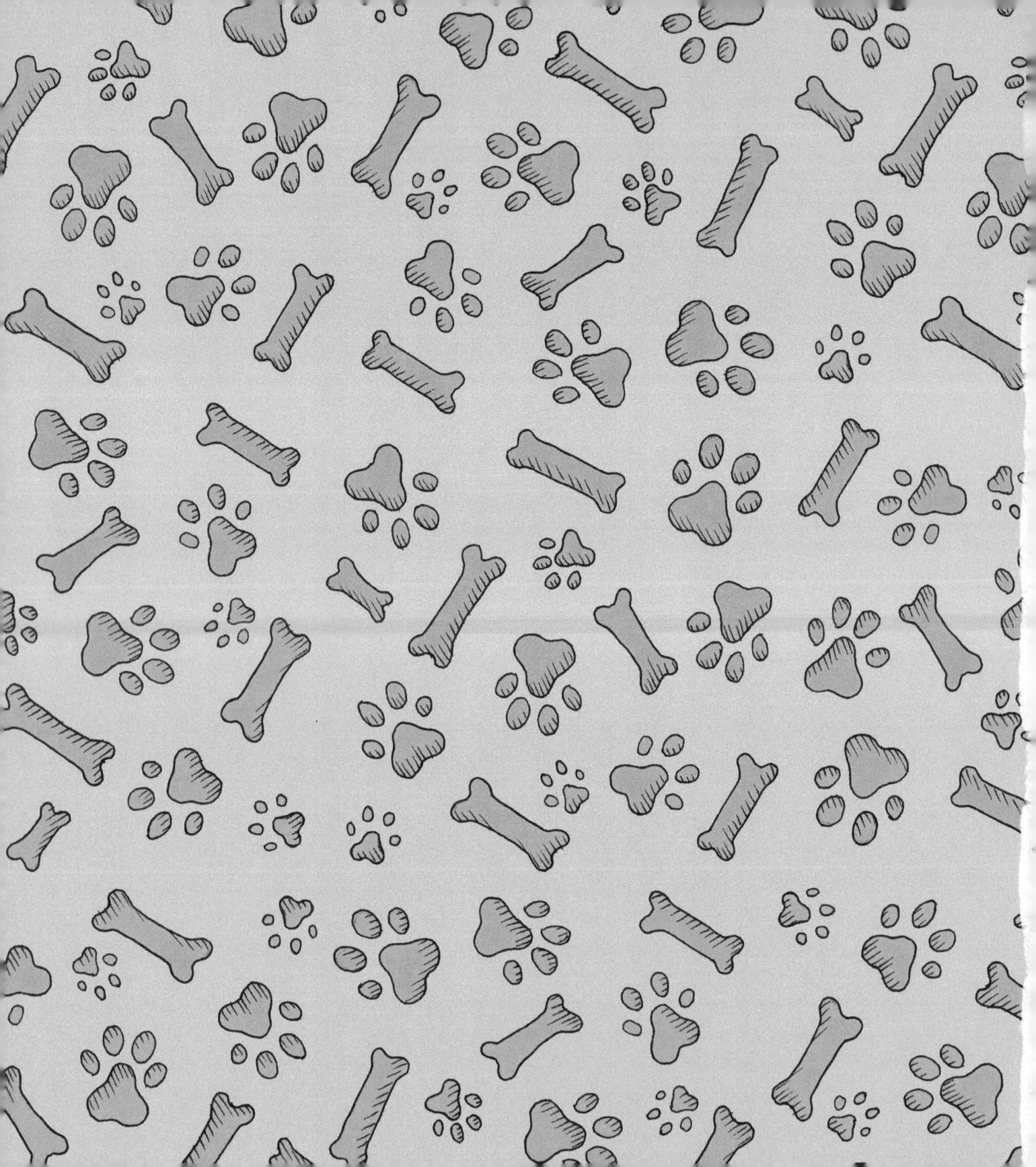

www.ingramcontent.com/pod-product-compliance
Lightning Source LLC
Chambersburg PA
CBHW061415090426

42742CB00026B/3474